Back a Winning Horse

Teach®
Yourself

Back a Winning Horse

Belinda Levez

For UK order enquiries: please contact Bookpoint Ltd,
130 Milton Park, Abingdon, Oxon OX14 4SB.
Telephone: +44 (0) 1235 827720. Fax: +44 (0) 1235 400454.
Lines are open 09.00–17.00, Monday to Saturday, with a 24-hour
message answering service. Details about our titles and how to
order are available at www.teachyourself.com

For USA order enquiries: please contact McGraw-Hill Customer
Services, PO Box 545, Blacklick, OH 43004-0545, USA.
Telephone: 1-800-722-4726. Fax: 1-614-755-5645.

For Canada order enquiries: please contact McGraw-Hill Ryerson
Ltd, 300 Water St, Whitby, Ontario L1N 9B6, Canada.
Telephone: 905 430 5000. Fax: 905 430 5020.

Long renowned as the authoritative source for self-guided learning –
with more than 50 million copies sold worldwide – the **Teach Yourself**
series includes over 500 titles in the fields of languages, crafts, hobbies,
business, computing and education.

British Library Cataloguing in Publication Data: a catalogue record
for this title is available from the British Library.

Library of Congress Catalog Card Number: on file.

First published in UK 1996 by Hodder Education, part of Hachette
UK, 338 Euston Road, London NW1 3BH.

First published in US 1996 by The McGraw-Hill Companies, Inc.

This edition published 2010.

Previously published as *Teach Yourself How to Win at Horse
Racing*.

The **Teach Yourself** name is a registered trade mark of Hodder
Headline.

Typeset by MPS Limited, A Macmillan Company.

Printed in Great Britain for Hodder Education, an Hachette UK
Company, 338 Euston Road, London NW1 3BH, by CPI Group
(UK) Ltd, Croydon, CR0 4YY.

The publisher has used its best endeavours to ensure that the URLs
for external websites referred to in this book are correct and active
at the time of going to press. However, the publisher and the
author have no responsibility for the websites and can make no
guarantee that a site will remain live or that the content will remain
relevant, decent or appropriate.

Hachette UK's policy is to use papers that are natural, renewable
and recyclable products and made from wood grown in sustainable
forests. The logging and manufacturing processes are expected to
conform to the environmental regulations of the country of origin.

Impression number   10 9 8 7 6 5 4 3 2
Year   2014 2013 2012

Contents

Meet the author

Welcome to *Back a Winning Horse*!

My name is Belinda Levez and I'll be your guide on this course of self-study, helping you to teach yourself how to back a winning horse. I am a former UK betting shop manager. I have also written many successful introductions to gambling. I have seen first-hand how bookmakers make their profits. They use many tricks that tempt gamblers to spend more money than they intended. Many people have learned from friends or family how to bet and have picked up some knowledge about horse racing. Often they have been misinformed. Some of these misconceptions contribute to gamblers losing money.

The most successful gamblers have a detailed knowledge of horse racing and betting. They can recognize when a bet is worthwhile and pick out horses that have the greatest chance of winning. They understand how a betting market works and know the rules. They can easily calculate their winnings and make an accurate assessment of the risks.

Throughout this book I will be sharing with you the inside knowledge that I have gained through my experience as a betting shop manager. Step-by-step, I will introduce you to the world of horse racing, helping you understand the jargon and the technical terms used. For those with little time I have included one-minute, five-minute and ten-minute summaries of the basic rules covered in the book.

Throughout the book you will find author insights that help to explain key points in greater detail. At the end of each chapter ten points are highlighted that you need to remember. I have also included a ready reckoner to help you easily calculate the winnings on your bets.

At the end of this course you should have a better understanding of horse racing and of betting. This will help you to make more informed choices about the type of bet you make and what you bet on.

Only got a minute?

Understanding the odds

When you place a bet, you will see that there are prices (odds) quoted for the runners. These prices are usually made up of two numbers with a slash between, for example 5/4, 11/8, 5/1, 7/2, 15/2, 25/1. These prices are a ratio telling you what you will win for a particular stake. The amount on the left of the price is what you will win if you bet the amount on the right. The money bet is called the stake. If you win, your stake is refunded, e.g. if the price quoted is 6/1, you will win £6 for every £1 staked. Your stake is also refunded. If you bet £5 on a horse at 6/1, your returns will be $(6 \times £5) + £5 = £35$.

How prices are determined

A bookmaker uses an expert called a handicapper to assess the chances of each runner in the race. The handicapper will consider a number of factors to determine the chances of each horse. Things like pedigree, recent performance, the jockey, weight carried and the condition of the ground will be taken into account. A book of prices is then made depending on the assessment. The runner that he thinks is most likely to win will have the lowest price and is called the favourite.

The initial prices offered are called tissue prices. This is a conservative estimate of a horse's chance of winning – a preliminary indication of the prices. Once bets have been made the prices are said to have been laid; this means that a betting market has been made. The prices then alter depending on how much is bet. The prices do not show the chances that a horse has of winning, they reflect how much money has been bet. The horse attracting the greatest amount of money will have the lowest price (the favourite); the horse attracting the least will have the highest price.

5 Only got five minutes?

Horse races are arranged into meets with a programme that will fill either a morning, afternoon or evening. Spending a day at the races is one of the most enjoyable aspects of betting on horse racing. You have the thrill of watching the race and are directly involved in the hustle and bustle of the betting ring.

For most meets, it is not necessary to book tickets. If you plan to attend a major race day, it is best to book in advance. On some race days members must wear morning dress and ladies are asked to wear hats. For most a jacket and tie is required in the members' enclosure.

Racecourses are divided into different areas, priced according to the facilities offered: the silver ring, tattersalls and the members' enclosure. Tattersalls is the main area, including the grandstand, paddock and winners' enclosure. The members' enclosure is the most expensive area and gives the best view of the course. It also offers access to tattersalls. The silver ring is the cheapest.

BEFORE AND DURING A RACE

Before a race, bets can be made when the bookmakers mark their boards and the tote screens display the approximate odds.

The jockeys are weighed before they rendezvous with the owners and trainers in the parade ring to receive last-minute instructions about how they should run.

A raised flag indicates that the race is about to begin. The announcer says, 'They're under orders.' When the starter is satisfied that the horses are ready, the announcer says, 'They're off.' At this point betting will stop. With long national hunt races, bookmakers may continue to accept bets after the off.

Jockey Club officials (stewards) watch the race to ensure that it is fairly run. The finish of each race is photographed and if it is close, the images will be scrutinised to determine the winner. The jockeys are weighed again, and if the stewards are satisfied, the announcement 'weighed in' will be given. Winning bets are then paid out. If a stewards' enquiry is announced, there will be a delay until it has been completed and one of the following announcements will be given:

- ▶ 'Result stands': the race was fairly run.
- ▶ 'Amended result': the rules have been broken.
- ▶ 'Race void': the stakes will be refunded to the punters.

BOOKMAKERS AND THE TOTE

In the silver ring and tattersalls the bookmakers cater for low-staking punters. Rails bookmakers are located in the rail that separates the tattersalls and the members' enclosure. They cater for high-staking punters, simply making a note of all bets placed. The range of bets offered by bookmakers is limited mostly to win and each-way.

Betting on the tote is a system where the total of the bets on a race are divided among those betting on the winner. This system is independent from bookmakers and any bets placed with bookmakers do not affect the winnings paid. At the racecourse a large board shows the number of bets placed on each runner, the total value of the bets and the payouts. If you have bet on a horse to win and it comes in first, you will have a share of the win pool. At the racecourse, you go to the tote or pari-mutuel counter and tell the member of staff the number of the horse you have selected, the type of bet you want and how much you want to stake. The advantage of betting on the tote is that you can bet for small stakes. The disadvantage with betting on the tote is that you do not know what your winnings will be.

10 Only got ten minutes?

Understanding the odds or prices is crucial to betting on horse racing. They provide an indication of your potential winnings and whether or not making a bet is worthwhile.

There is a huge variety of odds and prices and a lot of terms used to describe the odds. Sometimes you may take a price but conditions determine that this price is altered. The occurrence of dead heats, withdrawn horses and joint favourites may result in a lower payout than expected.

When you place a bet, you will see that there are prices (odds) quoted for the runners. These prices are made up of two numbers with a slash between, e.g. 5/4, 11/8. These prices are a ratio telling you what you will win for a particular stake. The amount on the left of the price is what you will win if you bet the amount on the right. The money bet is called the stake. If you win, your stake is refunded, e.g. if the price quoted is 6/1, you will win £6 for every £1 staked. Your stake is also refunded. If you bet £5 on a horse at 6/1, your returns will be (6 × £5) + £5 = £35.

Even though you may have taken a price, the odds at which your bet is settled may be adjusted if certain conditions apply, e.g.

▶ Non-runners – a horse that does not take part in the race. A horse may be withdrawn any time up to the off. If you bet on a non-runner on the day of the race, your stake will be refunded. If, however, you bet ante-post (before the day of the race), you will lose your stake.
▶ Withdrawn horses – after a book has been made on a race, a horse may be withdrawn. This will mean that the prices offered on the race will be incorrect, as they would have been worked out including the withdrawn horse. The bookmakers are therefore allowed to make an adjustment to the prices, called a 'rule 4 deduction' (R4).

- ► Each-way bets – withdrawn horses can also affect the odds paid and the number of places paid for each-way bets. If when you placed your bet there were eight runners, you would expect to be paid if your horse came third. However, if a horse is withdrawn, the third placed horse no longer counts, as there will only be seven runners. You will only be paid if your horse is first or second.
- ► Dead heats – occasionally, two horses or more are declared the winner. This is a dead heat. When a horse dead heats for first place, the returns are halved. If there are three horses in the dead heat, then the returns are divided by three.

Betting shops offer different types of prices and bets. They operate in a similar way to bookmakers by offering prices at fixed odds. Some of their prices are determined by what the on-course bookmakers are offering. Other prices are decided by the betting shops themselves. Types of price include:

- ► Ante-post prices – when a bet is placed before the day of the event it is called an 'ante-post' bet. For major races like the Grand National, prices are available many months before they are run. The prices are normally more favourable than those offered on the day of the event. However, if your runner is withdrawn from the race, your stake is automatically lost. Although ante-post betting has its risks, such as horses being withdrawn, the benefit of the higher prices is usually advantageous to the punter.
- ► Early morning prices – most betting shops offer prices on races as soon as they open for business. These are usually on the handicap races but some may give prices on all the races. These prices are quite often advertised in the sporting press.
- ► Starting prices – or 'SP' are an average of the prices that a sample of on-course bookmakers are offering at the start of the race, as agreed by the starting price executive. The starting price executive is made up of three major media companies, the Press Association, Trinity Mirror and Satellite Information Services. When the results of the races are published in the press, the starting prices will be quoted.

Ten minutes before the race starts the average prices will be passed from the bookmakers at the racecourse to betting shops. Once this information is received early morning prices can no longer be taken. Board prices will alter as money is bet. Each new set of prices that is transmitted is called a show. The first set of prices transmitted is called the first show. As the start of the race approaches prices will change. If you have taken an early price or ante-post price, then your bet will be settled at the odds taken, regardless of the starting price. If you do not take any of the prices previously mentioned, then your bet will be settled at the starting price.

The factors to consider when picking a winning horse are as follows:

▶ Pedigree – it is possible to trace the pedigree of a race horse back for hundreds of years. Horses are carefully bred to bring out characteristics that make good runners. Horses with good racing records are sent to stud in order to propagate those characteristics in future generations. However, the breeding of these characteristics is not an exact science. It tends to be used as a tool for finding winners where the horses have not run before.

▶ Previous performance – once the horse has run, you have a clearer indication of its potential. Information about how the horse has performed in previous races is known as 'form'. As the season progresses, you will have a better indication of how the horses are performing.

▶ Horses' speed – the speed that a horse can run is by far the clearest indication of how likely it is to win. No matter how good the jockey, the trainer or the condition of the ground, if a horse is not fast it is unlikely to win. Assessing the speed is not a simple matter. Factors such as the amount of weight carried and the going all affect a horse's speed.

▶ Distance of the race – most horses have an optimum distance over which they perform well. Some are sprinters while others have stamina to cope with longer distances. If a horse is entered for a distance that it has never run before, its previous performance can provide some indication as to how well it will fare.

- ▶ Change of class – the grade of race may have an effect on the outcome of a race, e.g. if a horse performs particularly well in a Class 2 race, it may be entered for a Class 1 race. Since Class 1 races attract the best horses, it will be up against much stronger opposition. Avoid betting on horses that have moved up a class, wait for them to prove themselves.
- ▶ Runners' experience – a horse's experience can be particularly important over jumps. A horse that has only recently been trained to jump is more likely to fall. Flat races where the horses start in stalls can cause problems. Experienced horses are more used to the stalls and less likely to be nervous.
- ▶ Condition of the ground ('the going') – the going is classified from the fastest to the slowest conditions as follows:
    - ▷ *hard*
    - ▷ *firm*
    - ▷ *good to firm*
    - ▷ *good*
    - ▷ *good to soft*
    - ▷ *soft/yielding*
    - ▷ *heavy*.
- ▶ Weather conditions – ground that started out as good can easily become heavy after a huge downpour. Some horses fare better than others depending on the weather conditions. Hot weather has an adverse effect on bigger horses.
- ▶ The course – in Great Britain all courses are different and this can have an effect on how well a horse runs.
- ▶ Condition of the horse – some horses have injury problems that make their performance unreliable. Keep up to date with the news to highlight any horses that are not entirely fit.
- ▶ The owner – some owners have a particularly good reputation for spotting and buying good-quality horses with the potential to win races.
- ▶ The trainer – some trainers have a good reputation for bringing out the very best in a horse.
- ▶ The jockey – over shorter distances the jockey is less crucial. With longer distances, experienced jockeys will generally fare better as tactics play a part in the outcome.

Introduction

You may already be betting on horse racing or have decided that you would like to have a bet. Many forms of gambling rely on pure luck. Horse racing differs. It is possible for a gambler to assess the runners in a race and to use his skill and judgement to predict the winner.

Many people gamble on horse racing with varying degrees of success. Some win money but a lot lose. Many of the losses could be avoided as they are often incurred owing to a lack of knowledge about horse racing and betting. Too many people rely on luck instead of skill.

Back a Winning Horse is a course of self-study that will help you to identify the factors that you need to consider when gambling on horse racing. It will help you to make better decisions based on the way that the industry works.

This book aims to teach you how to get better value. When you are gambling on horse racing you need to overcome the bookmaker's advantage. You will be shown how profitable the various bets are so that you can make an informed choice about those that are worth playing. You are also taught how to get the best price.

You are made aware of the ways in which bookmakers try to get you to spend more money. Advice is given on where to gamble. The dangers involved with betting illegally are highlighted.

By the end of the book you will be a more informed gambler with a better understanding of the subject and, it is to be hoped, a winner instead of a loser.

Good luck!

1

Horse racing

In this chapter you will learn:

- *about the origins of horse racing*
- *about the organization of horse racing*
- *about racing around the world.*

Origins of horse racing

Horse racing is a sport where two or more specially bred horses are raced around a track across a predetermined distance for a prize. It has existed for thousands of years, virtually since horses were first tamed and ridden. Chariot racing, the forerunner of harness racing, was probably the earliest form of the sport and was particularly popular in Ancient Greece and Rome. The first recorded mounted races were run in Ancient Greece.

Modern horse racing originated in England during the 12th century with the importation of Arab stallions. These horses, valued for their speed and stamina, were bred with English mares to produce racehorses. For the aristocracy, racing horses was a popular pastime. Early races were matches (two-horse races) for private bets. The competitors would race across country. Often church towers would be used as landmarks to denote the start and finish of a race. This led to the term steeplechase, which is still used today for jump races. In 1174 the Smithfield Track opened in London. Races were also held at fairs across the country.

Horse racing is known as the sport of kings. This title dates back to the time of King Charles II and stems from his interest in breeding and racing horses. This royal connection with horse racing continues today with Queen Elizabeth II who has a keen interest in the breeding and racing of horses.

During the 1700s racecourses opened all over England and transformed horse racing into a professional sport. In 1750 an organization called the Jockey Club was formed to control and administer English racing. The Jockey Club laid down the rules of racing and classified races. In 1814 five races considered to be the most challenging were designated the classics and survive to the present day. These are the Derby, the Oaks, the 1000 Guineas, the 2000 Guineas and the St Leger. Gradually the value of the purses (prizes) increased, making the racing and breeding of horses a profitable pastime.

Horse racing was introduced to America when the country was first settled. English immigrants brought thoroughbred horses with them and in 1665 a racetrack was established on Long Island. In common with England, races were designated as classics. Horse racing rose in popularity and by 1890 there were 314 racetracks. However, corruption was rife. To combat this the American Jockey Club was formed in 1894. It was modelled on the English Jockey Club and laid down rules to ensure that horse racing was fair. However, a ban on bookmaking resulted in the decline of horse racing and by 1908 only 25 tracks survived. The introduction of pari-mutuel betting for the Kentucky Derby in 1908 led to a revival. In return for a share of the profits from betting, more and more states legalized pari-mutuel betting. This system continues today.

Thoroughbred horses

The Jockey Club allocated James Weatherby the task of tracing the pedigree of every racehorse in England. In 1791 he published the *Introduction to the General Stud Book*. To the present day, details of every thoroughbred foal born in England are recorded in the *General Stud Book*. By the early 1800s only horses listed in the *General Stud Book* were allowed to race. As horse racing developed around the world, other countries began their own stud books. *The American Stud Book*, recording the pedigree of all thoroughbred race horses foaled, was started in 1868.

Horses listed in the *General Stud Book* are called thoroughbreds. A thoroughbred is a horse descended from one of three stallions, the Darley Arabian (1724), the Godolphin Arabian (1724) and the Byerley Turk (1680). Thoroughbred horses compete in flat and national hunt/steeplechase racing. The date of birth of thoroughbreds is 1 January, regardless of when they were actually born. They begin their training as yearlings when they learn to accept a saddle, bridle and rider. They are then trained to go into the starting stalls and run around a track. They usually begin their racing careers as 2-year-olds. Although their peak racing age is 5 years, those with excellent winning records are often retired earlier to go to stud.

Types of racing

FLAT RACING

Flat racing refers to the fact that no jumping is involved. The actual racecourses are rarely flat as many tracks have uphill or downhill slopes. The races tend to be short with many sprints. The length of the races varies from short sprints of around 5 furlongs (1005 metres) to longer races of around 2 miles (3.2 km). In the United States, races tend to be shorter and are between 5 and 12 furlongs. Races take place on a variety of surfaces including turf, dirt, sand and fibre-sand, which is a manmade material.

Starting stalls are used to start flat races to ensure a fair outcome. The starting stalls is a mechanical device that ensures all the horses start the race at the same time. Each compartment of the stalls has doors at the front and the back. The horses are loaded into the back and the doors are closed behind them. When all the horses are loaded, the doors at the front open simultaneously at the off. A draw takes place to determine which stall each runner starts from.

NATIONAL HUNT OR STEEPLECHASES

National hunt races or steeplechases are particularly popular in Great Britain, Ireland and France. This type of racing originated from fox hunting. The races are held over obstacles such as brush fences, wooden rails, stone walls and water-filled ditches. The obstacles vary in size from hurdles of around 1 to 2 feet (30–60cm) to the enormous Grand National fences. Jumpers generally compete over hurdles before graduating to the larger obstacles. Hurdle races are for horses aged 3 years after 1 July. National hunt races are run over longer distances than flat races and are usually started with a starting gate or by flag. The hurdle races start from 2 miles. Steeplechases can be as long as 4½ miles.

The horses taking part in steeplechases tend to be bigger and older than those competing in flat racing. They are specially bred to give a combination of size, speed and stamina. The horses start racing from the age of 4 years after 1 July. It is not unusual for the horses to continue racing until they are 10 or older. Red Rum, for example, was 12 years old when he won the Grand National for the third time.

There are also some races for national hunt horses that have no obstacles. They are called national hunt flat races and are run across national hunt courses. These races are for horses aged between 4 and 6 years old that have not raced in any other official races.

HARNESS RACING

Modern harness racing originated in the United States during the 18th century when it was a popular pastime for individuals to race each other over country roads. The country's fairs became a major venue for organized races. The first racetracks were established at the beginning of the 19th century. In 1939 the United States

Trotting Association was established. It is responsible for the registration of standardbreds (the horses) and keeping records of each horse's racing career. After 1900 harness racing declined mainly due to the introduction of the automobile. In 1940 Roosevelt Raceway in New York introduced floodlit harness racing with pari-mutuel betting which boosted the popularity of the sport. Nowadays harness racing is found all over the United States and is particularly popular in the Midwest and East. Harness racing is also found in continental Europe, Canada, Australia and New Zealand.

Harness racing is run on an oval-shaped dirt track. Most races are 1 mile long and are usually run anti-clockwise. The jockey, called a driver, sits in the harness called a sulky or racebike. The horses must trot and are disqualified if they break into a gallop for too long. If a horse breaks into a gallop, the driver must bring the horse back to its correct gait and lose ground to the other competitors.

STANDARDBRED HORSES

Standardbred horses compete in harness racing. They are smaller than thoroughbreds and more muscular with a long body and bigger head. Standardbred horses originated in the 1780s from an English thoroughbred, Messenger, which was exported to the US. One of its descendants was Hambletonian 10, from which all standardbred horses are descended. These horses are so called because the early trotters had to reach a certain standard over the mile distance to gain registration as a standardbred. They start racing as 2- or 3-year-olds.

There are two types of standardbred – trotters and pacers. The difference between them is in the way they move. Pacers are faster than trotters and make up around 80 per cent of harness racers. Often called sidewheelers, they move with the legs on one side of their body in unison (front right and back right together, and front left and back left together). Pacers are fitted with plastic loops called hobbles, which are an aid to maintaining the correct gait. If a horse runs without hobbles it is called free legged.

Trotters move with a diagonal gait (front right and back left together, and front left and back right together).

Trotting races are usually started from a standing position. Pacing races are generally started with a moving start. A starting gate is attached to a vehicle. When the judge is satisfied that the horses are all level with the gate, the vehicle accelerates away.

Grading of races

There is a hierarchy of races. The more prestigious a race, the higher its purse. In Great Britain, flat races are graded into seven classes with Class 1 being the highest and 7 the lowest.

The rating of a horse determines which class it races in. Its rating is calculated by a team of six handicappers appointed by the British Horse Racing Board. They assess the performance of each horse by watching races live and viewing the stewards' tapes of the races. They give each horse a rating on a scale of 0 to 140, the latter being the highest. The top horses are those with a rating over 110 and they compete in the best races.

Insight

Generally a horse needs to run in three races before it is given a rating. The ratings are published every Tuesday on the British Horse Racing Authority's website. An average rating for a horse competing in flat races is 60, for jumping it is about 95.

The classification of flat races has undergone a number of changes in recent years. After the 2004 season, the system was changed to incorporate seven classes as follows:

Class 1: *pattern and listed races (including those handicaps 96–110)*
Class 2: *heritage handicaps, 91–105 and 86–100*
Class 3: *81–95, 76–90*

Class 4: *71–85, 66–80*
Class 5: *61–75, 56–70*
Class 6: *51–65, 46–60 and 46–55*
Class 7: *regional racing.*

The national hunt races are divided into grades as follows:

Grades 1, 2, 3
Grade 1 novice
Grade 2 novice
Grade 1 NHF (national hunt flat)
Grade 2 NHF
Grades B to H inclusive.

Insight

If a horse wins a race and runs again before its new rating has been calculated it will carry extra weight in its next race – 6 pounds for flat races and 8 pounds for jumps. This is called a penalty.

In the United States the stakes races are divided into groups. Group numbers are denoted by roman numerals. Group I races are the highest and Group III the lowest. With harness racing they are grouped as A, B and C with Group A races the highest and Group C the lowest. Other races are ungraded, and include claiming races where the horses competing in the race may be purchased by registered owners at a set price. Ownership of the horse changes as soon as the race is off. Allowance races are for apprentice jockeys where the jockeys are allowed to claim a weight allowance.

Handicaps

A handicap is a race where the chances of all the competitors winning are evened out by handicapping them with extra weight. If the handicapper does his job correctly all the horses should cross the line at the same time. The horses that are deemed to have the best chances of winning are required to carry the greatest amount of weight. The weight is added by means of lead bars that are inserted into the saddle. The jockeys are weighed with their saddles both before and after the race to ensure that they are carrying the correct weight. Occasionally these weights can fall off in the course of the race. This leads to disqualification of the horse.

Insight

Handicap races enable slower horses to compete in races with faster horses. Suppose one horse is rated 120 and another rated 110. In a handicap race the horse rated 120 would carry 10 pounds in weight to give the other horse an equal chance of winning the race.

Conditional races

For many races there are conditions placed on entry. There may be age restrictions, for example, races for 2-year-old or 3-year-old horses. Others may be for apprentice jockeys or women jockeys or amateur riders. Races may be for maidens – horses that have never won before. In Great Britain, there are selling races where the winner is auctioned after the race.

Gambling on horse racing

Gambling on horse racing started virtually as soon as horse racing was invented. The matches would often be subject to a private wager or gentlemen's agreement. With the organization of racecourses came bookmakers who would act as a banker and agree to cover everyone's bets. However, their actions were often far from gentlemanly and they were notorious for welshing on bets. This led to many countries either outlawing bookmakers or introducing legislation that governed the way in which they could operate. Some countries also introduced state-operated betting to ensure that betters would get a fair deal.

HOW FAIR IS BETTING?

In many countries betting operations are state controlled to safeguard the public against unscrupulous operators.

Most countries have introduced some form of gambling legislation to set out the conditions under which betting on horse racing is allowed.

In the UK, the relevant legislation is the Gambling Act 2005, which was introduced to modernize UK gambling law. The Gambling Commission is responsible for regulating gambling. Bookmakers are required to be licensed. In order to gain a permit a bookmaker must show that he or she is a fit and proper person. Regulations also determine when and how a bookmaker can operate his or her business.

INTERNET AND TELEPHONE BETTING

Care needs to be taken when gambling on the internet as there are many unregulated sites in foreign jurisdictions. Some governments have introduced strict controls for sites operating in their countries. UK sites are regulated by the Gambling Commission and Australian sites are government regulated. In the USA, there are state-regulated betting sites.

The internet has opened up a host of betting opportunities. Internet betting is wagering via a computer over an internet connection. This allows you to bet from the comfort of your home, 24 hours a day. You can bet on virtually any horse racing event in the world including racing in the UK, USA and Australia. There are four main types of operator that offer remote betting: bookmakers, the tote, betting exchanges and spread betting firms. There are major differences in each method.

Although internet betting offers greater convenience to the customer, it does need to be treated with caution as there are a number of scam sites and sites that have gone bust owing customers money. Be extremely cautious of betting with unregulated sites in foreign jurisdictions. If a site goes bust it will be virtually impossible for you to get your money back.

THE LAW

Depending on where you live, internet betting may or may not be legal. As the legal situation may change at any time, you are advised to check the legality of internet betting in your jurisdiction before placing any bets.

In the both the United States and Great Britain, gambling debts are not recoverable at law. In Great Britain, an organization has been set up to resolve punters' disputes with bookmakers. The Independent Betting Arbitration Service (IBAS) was established in 1998. It offers a free arbitration service to customers of bookmakers who are registered with it. Bookmakers in the scheme have agreed to co-operate with any investigations into their operations and to abide by decisions made by IBAS. If a bookmaker fails to abide by the scheme, he may have renewal of his betting permit refused.

HOW FAIR IS RACING?

The various controlling bodies of racing go to great lengths to ensure that racing is fair. For example in Great Britain, where the Jockey Club administers horse racing, there are strict controls in place. The Jockey Club is actively involved in detecting any form of foul play by gathering intelligence, carrying out surveillance and monitoring moves in the betting market. If they suspect foul play, they investigate the matter and pass their findings on to the police. The Jockey Club is also responsible for racecourse security and uses CCTV at racecourse stables. The Jockey Club also appoints stewards who ensure that the rules of racing are followed. At each race meeting the stewards watch the races live. They also have access to all the tape recordings of races made at vantage points around the course. If there is an infringement of the rules they have the power to amend the result, disqualify runners or void a race.

Britain bans the use of performance-enhancing drugs in horse racing. Programmes are in place to test horses for doping. Each year around 10 per cent of horses are dope tested. The incidence of horses being tested positive is extremely low.

In the past race fixers would substitute a horse for a ringer (a horse of similar appearance that has a greater chance of winning). This has been combatted by issuing all thoroughbred race horses, registered in the General Stud Book, with passports at birth. This document includes details of their pedigree, colour and distinguishing markings. Random checks are carried out at racecourses to verify the identity of horses. In addition, blood samples can be taken and analysed and compared with those taken from the horse on registration. From 1 January 1999 thoroughbreds were microchipped. A microchip inserted into the horse's neck can be scanned to confirm the horse's identity.

A day at the races

Spending a day at the races is one of the most enjoyable aspects of betting on horse racing. You have the thrill of watching the race at close quarters as the horses thunder along the rails and are directly involved in the hustle and bustle of the betting ring as bets are laid.

Horse races are arranged into meetings with a programme of racing that will fill either a morning, afternoon or evening. Races are generally timed to take place at roughly 30-minute intervals.

PLANNING YOUR DAY

Information about forthcoming meetings is advertised in the racing newspapers. For most meetings, it is not necessary to book tickets. You simply pay on arrival at the course. If you plan to attend a major race day, it is best to book tickets in advance, particularly for the more expensive areas of the course. Also, check the dress code. On some race days members are required to wear morning dress and ladies are asked to wear hats. For most other race days smart dress of jacket and tie is a necessary requirement for men in the members' area. Make sure you are wearing comfortable shoes, as you are likely to do a lot of walking.

Before you start your journey to a race meeting always check that the racing is still going ahead, particularly if the weather is bad. Frost, snow, heavy fog or waterlogged tracks can all be reasons for a meeting being abandoned. You can find up-to-date information on the internet, teletext services, radio and television broadcasts.

Allow plenty of time for your journey and bear in mind that there may be heavy traffic near the racecourse. If you are using public transport, you will often find that extra buses are laid on. Aim to arrive at least an hour before the first race starts. This will give you enough time to find your way around all the facilities.

Racecourses are divided up into different areas, which are priced according to the facilities offered. They are the silver ring, tattersalls and the members' enclosure. Tattersalls, usually referred to as tatts, is the main area, which includes the grandstand, paddock and winners' enclosure. The members' enclosure is the most expensive area and gives the best view of the course, particularly of the winning post. You will be issued with a badge, which you should wear to gain access to all the facilities. Spectators in the members' enclosure also gain access to tattersalls. The silver ring is the cheapest area. It is so called because it used to cost less than a pound for admission. Each area of the racecourse will have a range of catering facilities including restaurants, bars and fast-food outlets.

The grandstand provides seating for spectators and gives a good view of the racecourse. Giant television screens give further coverage of the races. During the course of the race, a commentary is given via loud speakers. The paddock is where the horses are paraded before racing. Here the owners give last-minute instructions to the jockeys before they mount their horses and ride down to the start of the race. For major races the horses are often paraded on the racecourse in front of the grandstand. The winners' enclosure is where the winning and placed horses are displayed at the end of the race. There is a podium here, which is used for presenting prizes.

THE RUNNING OF A RACE

The clerk of the course is the person responsible for the running of the racecourse. Before racing, he will inspect the course and declare the official going.

Before the start of the race, betting commences with both the bookmakers and the tote. The bookmakers mark their tissue prices on their boards and the tote screens begin to display the approximate odds.

The weighing room is where the jockeys are weighed both before and after the race to ensure that their weight has not changed. The jockeys are all weighed and proceed to the parade ring where they rendezvous with the owners and trainers. The jockey's receive last-minute instructions about how they should run the race. The horses are led to the parade ring by stable staff and are saddled. Around five minutes before the off, the jockeys mount the horses and ride down to the start. The announcer will say, 'They're going down.'

The starter will often indicate that he is ready to start the race by raising a flag. The announcer will say, 'They're under orders.' When the starter is satisfied that the horses are ready to start the race, it will be declared off. The announcer will say, 'They're off.' As soon as the race is off, betting stops. This will often be accompanied by a ringing bell to indicate that betting has stopped. With long national hunt races, some bookmakers may continue to accept bets for a short while after the off or until a horse falls. Occasionally there may be a false start and the horses will be recalled.

Commentary will be given about the race. A number of Jockey Club officials called stewards watch the races to ensure that they are fairly run. The race is also recorded via a number of cameras set at different vantage points along the track.

The finish of each race is photographed and if it is particularly close, the film will be developed and scrutinised to determine the winner. The race result will be announced. The winning and placed horses are ridden to the winners' enclosure. The jockeys then proceed to the weighing room to weigh in. If the stewards are satisfied that the race was fairly run, the announcement 'weighed in' will be given. Winning bets are then paid out. If a stewards' enquiry or objection is announced, there will be a delay in giving the 'weighed-in' announcement and in paying out the winning bets until the incident leading to the enquiry or objection has been fully investigated.

Insight

A stewards' enquiry can be called for various reasons, including excessive use of the whip, taking the wrong course, impeding another horse, a false start, or a discrepancy in the weights.

After the investigation an announcement of 'result stands', 'amended result' or 'race void' will be given. 'Result stands' means that the stewards are satisfied that the race was fairly run. 'Amended result' means that the stewards have decided that the rules of racing have been broken. They may disqualify a competitor or declare a different winner or placed horses. If the race is declared void, stakes will be refunded to the punters. Later, a short ceremony is held to present the prizes and trophies won for the race.

IDENTIFYING THE RUNNERS

Each horse has a number marked on its saddlecloth that corresponds to its number on the race card. The vast majority of race horses are varying shades of brown, which makes them difficult to identify at a distance. To help spectators identify their horses, the jockeys wear silks, which are brightly coloured shirts, and cap covers. Owners have their own colours, which are registered. Details of the colours worn by each jockey are given on the race card. Binoculars are useful for watching the runners at a distance. If you don't have your own, it is possible to hire them from the racecourse for a small fee.

Insight

The race card number is the number that will be marked on the saddle cloth. Don't confuse the race card number with the draw. The draw is the position that the horse will start in the starting stalls in a flat race.

Owning a racehorse

An added thrill to betting on horse racing is owning your own horse. Nowadays you do not have to be wealthy to own a racehorse. It is possible to buy a share in a horse through partnerships and clubs. Costs vary from between £3500 and £50,000 per share. Details of partnerships and clubs are advertised in the horse-racing media.

Due to the high prize money paid, Hong Kong is one of the most profitable places to run a horse. Purses are equivalent to around four times those paid in the UK. Around 47 per cent of the horses in Hong Kong earn enough to cover their costs. A successful horse can be highly profitable. Owners invested HK$325,000 in a horse called Quicken Away and won HK$8.75 million (US$1.1 million) in prizes.

Racing around the world

GREAT BRITAIN

The British Horse Racing Board governs racing in Great Britain. There are 59 racecourses, which are all different. Most races take place on turf. Three racecourses have fibre-sand tracks, which allow racing to go ahead in adverse weather conditions. These are Lingfield Park, Southwell and Wolverhampton. On average, there are three to four race meetings taking place daily. Flat racing dominates in spring and summer, with national hunt racing during autumn and winter. There is no harness racing except for a few novelty events. Racing takes place all year round with the exception of Christmas Day and Good Friday.

Britain has legal independent on-course bookmakers and tote betting. There are also on-course betting shops where it is also possible to bet on races at other meetings. In addition, there are 8500 off-course betting shops, which show live racing via satellite on television screens. The off-course shops take bets on the average odds offered by the on-course bookmakers, tote bets and offer telephone-betting facilities in the form of deposit and credit accounts.

Main events of the racing calendar

The most important races are the classics for 3-year-olds – 2000 Guineas, 1000 Guineas, the Derby, Oaks and St Leger. The 2000 Guineas and 1000 Guineas are run over the Rowley Mile Course at Newmarket in May. The Derby and the Oaks are staged at Epsom Downs. The Derby, which was first run in 1780, attracts the best horses from around the world. It is a 1½ mile race for 3-year-old colts with over £1 million in prize money. The Oaks is the Derby's counterpart for fillies. The St Leger is the world's oldest classic and is held at Doncaster in September. A horse that wins the 2000 Guineas, Derby and St Leger in the same year gains the Triple Crown title.

Other major flat races include the Gold Cup and the Spring Double. The Gold Cup, a race over 2½ miles, is the premier race of the Royal Ascot meeting. First held in 1807, it is run on the third day of the meeting. The Spring Double is the name given to the Lincolnshire and the Grand National. The Autumn Double is the Cesarewitch and the Cambridgeshire. The Cesarewitch is a handicap held in late October at Newmarket. The race dates from 1839 and was named to honour the state visit of Russian prince, Alexander II. (*Tzarevich* is the Russian word for heir to the throne.)

The most famous national hunt race is the Grand National, which is a steeplechase handicap run at Aintree in April. The race, first run in 1839, is a true test of endurance with the horses competing over a distance of 4 miles and 856 yards. Just completing the course without falling is a huge challenge. In 1928, only two horses managed to finish. There are 30 fences to be jumped, all of which are notoriously difficult, especially Beecher's Brook and Valentine's Brook, which are water jumps. The Grand National holds the record for the most runners in a race – in 1929, 66 horses competed.

Other major national hunt races include the Cheltenham Festival and the King George VI & Queen Elizabeth Diamond Stakes. The Cheltenham festival is the premier national hunt meeting and is held in March. It features the Champion Hurdle and the Cheltenham Gold Cup. Kempton Park hosts the King George VI & Queen Elizabeth Diamond Stakes on Boxing Day (26 December).

IRELAND

The Irish Turf Club, established in 1790, controls racing in Ireland. A new body created in 1994, the Irish Horse Racing Authority, is responsible for administering government grants to the industry. Ireland has a thriving stud farm industry and is world renowned for the breeding of horses.

There are 27 major racecourses. All are turf except for Laytown where races are run on the sandy beach. A mixture of flat and jump meetings are held. Racing takes place 7 days a week.

There is on-course betting with bookmakers, which is tax free, as well as tote betting. There are also 900 off-course betting shops with betting on both Irish and British racing, which is televised via satellite.

The Curragh is the headquarters of flat racing, staging all five classic races: the Irish Derby, the Irish 1000 and 2000 Guineas, the Irish Oaks and the Irish St Leger.

Leopardstown in the major national hunt venue. It also hosts flat meetings and in September it stages the Champion Stakes, which is a World Series of Racing event. The course is also host to the Irish Gold Cup in February.

Ireland has five major festivals of racing – Galway, Listowel, Tralee, Killarney and the Derby Festival at the Curragh. At the festival meetings, racing takes place for between 3 and 7 days. Galway is the most famous, lasting for 7 days. In addition to the racing, there are lots of other entertainment activities including live music, exhibitions, fairs and competitions.

UNITED STATES OF AMERICA

In the United States racing is controlled by state racing commissions. They are responsible for the issuing of licences and approving racing fixtures. Together with the Jockey Club, they appoint racing officials and ensure racing rules are adhered to. Racing takes place all year round. Meetings often last for over ten weeks. There are over 500 racetracks, which vary little – all tend to be oval-shaped dirt tracks with left-hand bends. The emphasis is on speed, with lots of short races. The US Trotting Association promotes harness racing, which is more popular than thoroughbred racing with more tracks and more races each year. National hunt racing is only found at a few meetings. It is regulated by the National Steeplechase and Hunt Association.

On-course betting is via the pari-mutuel system, although it is estimated that betting with illegal bookmakers far exceeds betting on the tote. In some states, there is legal off-course betting. These include Arizona, Connecticut, Illinois, Louisiana, Nebraska, Nevada, New York, North Dakota, Oregon, Pennsylvania, Washington State and Wyoming.

Main events of the racing calendar

The US classics are the Belmont Stakes, the Preakness Stakes and the Kentucky Derby. Each race makes up one leg of the Triple Crown. The Kentucky Derby, first run in 1875, is held at Churchill Downs near Louisville, Kentucky. It is run over 1¼ miles on the first Saturday of May. This race forms the first leg of the Triple Crown. The Preakness Stakes dates from 1873. It is held at Pimlico and is run over 1³⁄₁₆ miles. The Belmont Stakes was first run in 1867. Throughout its history the race was run over various distances. It is now run over 1½ miles. It takes place five weeks after the Kentucky Derby at Belmont Park in Belmont, New York.

Other major races include the Breeders' Cup Classic and Turf and the Arlington Million. These races form part of the World Series of Racing. The Breeders' Cup races are held at Churchill Downs in Louisville, Kentucky during late October or early November. The Breeders' Cup Turf is run over 1½ miles with a $2 million prize. The Breeders' Cup Classic is over 1¼ miles for a prize of $4 million. The Arlington Million, which is held at Arlington Park in Chicago, was the first race to offer a $1 million prize. The race over 1¼ miles on turf is now worth $2 million.

The Breeders' Cup Steeplechase is held at Far Hills, New Jersey. Horses of 4 years and up compete over 2⅝ miles for the country's largest steeplechase prize. Three of the country's oldest steeplechase races are still run today: the Maryland Cup (1894), the American Grand National (1899) and the National Hunt Cup (1909).

In harness racing, the richest race is the Hambletonian. The race for 3-year-olds is held at Meadowlands Racetrack in East Rutherford, New Jersey. It has a purse of over $1 million. The race takes its name from the stallion, Hambletonian, which was born in Orange County, New York, on 5 May 1849. As a 3-year-old it trotted a mile in 2 minutes 48½ seconds. It was put to stud and sired 1331 foals, including Dexter, which became a world champion trotter in 1867. The Hambletonian, Yonkers' Trot and the Kentucky Futurity make up the trotting Triple Crown. The pacers Triple Crown is the Little Brown Jug, the Messenger Stakes and the Cane Pace.

CONTINENTAL EUROPE

There is horse racing across most of continental Europe dominated by harness racing. In eastern Europe, the Netherlands and Belgium, the introduction of satellite technology has resulted in a large amount of betting taking place on foreign racing (mostly British and Irish). In eastern Europe, betting is via casinos and cafes on the tote. Belgium has on-course bookmakers, tote and off-course betting shops. Italy has off-course betting shops, which allow betting on the tote. In Scandinavian countries, betting is via the tote. European operators have also innovated a system of commingling tote pools, which creates potentially bigger payouts.

FRANCE

France has a state-run horse racing industry controlled by the National Federation of French Racing. There are 260 racecourses with a mixture of flat, steeplechase and harness racing. Bookmakers are illegal so betting is on the state-run tote (the PMU or pari-mutuel). Bets may be placed on-course or in betting shops and cafes. A recent change has been the innovation of off-course race-by-race betting. The trifecta and superfecta bets are particularly popular.

The French classics are the Prix du Jockey Club (1836), the Grand Prix du Paris (1863) and the Prix de l'Arc de Triomphe (1920). Longchamp, just outside Paris, plays host to the Prix de l'Arc de Triomphe, which is Europe's richest race with a prize of €2.25 million (roughly $1.5 million).

AUSTRALIA

In Australia, there is racing all year round. Australia has 380 racecourses that are mostly turf. There is a mixture of racing including flat racing, which is called gallops, and steeplechase races. Harness racing is particularly popular and is generally referred to as the trots. There are 206 clubs that organize races.

Betting is with on-course bookmakers and tote betting. Tote bets can also be placed at off-course betting shops, pubs, casinos and over the telephone. Popular bets are the quinella (reversed forecast) place and the tierce or trifecta (tricast). The quinella place is selecting any two of the first three placed horses in any order.

The Melbourne Cup is a race that dates from 1861. It is traditionally held on the first Tuesday in November at the Flemington Race Course. It is Australia's richest race with a purse of AU$3 million (roughly US$2 million). The Cox Plate is held in October at Moonee Valley, Melbourne. Runners compete on turf, over 2040 metres, for a prize of AU$1 million. The Miracle Mile is Australia's richest pacing race.

NEW ZEALAND

Horse racing in New Zealand is governed by the Racing Industry Board and operated by individual clubs. There are 155 clubs that organize race meetings at 71 racetracks. There is thoroughbred racing on turf and harness racing on mostly all-weather surfaces (around 10 per cent of or harness racing is on turf). Betting is controlled by the TAB and is available both on and off course on either the tote or fixed odds. There are 510 off-course betting outlets run by the TAB. The TAB also operates telephone betting services and an internet site.

SOUTH AFRICA

South Africa has 15 racetracks. The tracks are owned and operated by race clubs. Betting is with the tote, on-course bookmakers and off-course tote outlets. There is also telephone betting.

Major races include the Summer Handicap and the July. The Summer Handicap is the country's richest. It is held in November at Turffontein Race Course in Johannesburg. Horses of 3 years old and up compete over 2000 metres for a R1.2 million prize (approximately $156,000). The July, a race dating from 1897, takes place at Greyville racetrack in Durban. It is run on the first Saturday of July over a distance of 2200 metres for a prize of R1 million (around $130,500).

CANADA

Horse racing in Canada is governed by the Canadian Pari-Mutuel Association. Each province has a racing commission, which is responsible for ensuring the rules of racing are adhered to. Canada has 40 racetracks offering both thoroughbred and harness racing. Betting is via the pari-mutuel and includes betting on US racing. The Canadian International, part of the World Series of Racing, is held at Woodbine Racetrack in October. Three-year-olds and up compete over 1 mile 4 furlongs (1½ miles) for a purse of $1.5 million. Other major races include the Molson Mile, the Queen's Plate, the Western Canada Derby Series and the Gold Cup and Saucer.

JAPAN

Japan has 37 racecourses with tote betting, off-course betting outlets and telephone betting facilities. The races are organized by the JRA and local government. The top horses (around 6500) are registered with the JRA, which organizes races at ten courses across Japan. The Japan Cup, part of the World Series of Racing, is held at Tokyo Race course in November. Three-year-olds and up compete over 2400 metres (about 1½ miles) on turf for a purse of over $4.5 million.

HONG KONG

Hong Kong has two racecourses – Sha Tin and Happy Valley. Happy Valley dates from 1846 and hosts a programme of races from September to June. Sha Tin is the venue for prestigious international events including the Hong Kong Cup, which is part of the World Series and takes place in December. Three-year-olds and up compete over 2000 metres (10 furlongs) for a purse of $1.8 million.

WORLD SERIES RACING CHAMPIONSHIP

In common with other sports, it was decided to organize a World
Series championship for horse racing. The first event took place
in 1999. Horses may compete in races held across four continents.
The competition features some of the world's most prestigious
races. The first race in the series is the Dubai World Cup, run
over 1¼ miles on dirt, at the Nad Al Sheba Racecourse in Dubai
in the United Arab Emirates. With a prize of $6 million it is the
world's richest race. It was established in 1996 and is viewed in
over 197 countries. The other qualifying races are the King George
VI & Queen Elizabeth Diamond Stakes, the Arlington Million, the
Grosser Preis von Baden, the Irish Champion Stakes, the Canadian
International, the Cox Plate, the Breeders' Cup Classic, Breeders'
Cup Turf, Japan Cup and the Hong Kong Cup. The first six
horses in each race are allocated points based on the system
used for Formula 1 Grand Prix as follows:

first place: 12 points *fourth place: 3 points*
second place: 6 points *fifth place: 2 points*
third place: 4 points *sixth place: 1 point.*

10 THINGS TO REMEMBER

1 There are different types of racing including flat racing, national hunt and harness racing.

2 Thoroughbred horses compete in flat and national hunt racing.

3 Standardbred horses compete in harness racing.

4 The British classics are the 2000 Guineas, 1000 Guineas, the Derby and the Oaks. The US classics are the Belmont Stakes, the Preakness Stakes and the Kentucky Derby.

5 British races are graded into seven classes with Class 1 being the highest and 7 the lowest.

6 US races are divided into groups denoted by roman numerals. Group I races are the highest and Group III the lowest.

7 Harness races are grouped as A, B and C with Group A races the highest and Group C the lowest.

8 British horses are rated on a scale of 0 to 140, the latter being the highest.

9 A handicap is a race where the chances of all the competitors winning are evened out by handicapping them with extra weight.

10 The horses can be identified by the numbers on their saddlecloths which correspond to the race card number.

2

Racecourse betting

In this chapter you will learn:
- *about on-course bookmakers*
- *about tote and pari-mutuel betting*
- *how to understand the odds.*

On-course bookmakers

Bookmaking is a system of betting on fixed odds or prices. Bookmakers are independent operators who take bets on horse racing. This system of betting exists alongside the tote. Unlike the tote, the money bet does not go into a pool. Instead, the customer bets against the individual bookmaker at odds that are agreed at the time the bet is placed. It is much like a bet between two individuals. This means that when you place your bet with a bookmaker, you can immediately calculate how much you could win.

A number of countries including Great Britain, Ireland, Belgium, Australia and South Africa have legal bookmakers. They carry out their business at the racecourse in designated areas. Some countries do not allow bookmaking at all.

In the silver ring and tattersalls each bookmaker is allocated a pitch or stand. They advertise the prices they are offering on each horse on boards or electronic displays. For each race, the horses' names, race card number and odds offered are marked. These bookmakers cater for low-staking punters.

Rails bookmakers are located in a separate area, usually along the rail that separates the members' enclosure from tattersalls. They take bets from high-staking punters, other bookmakers and credit customers. Their prices are not advertised on boards; instead, they simply make a note of all bets placed.

The range of bets offered by bookmakers is limited mostly to win and each-way bets. When you have selected a bookmaker, tell him your selection, the type of bet you want and your stake. You can either just call out the price on offer or announce the returns to the stakes. Suppose you wanted to bet £8 on Dobbin to win at 6/1. You can simply announce '£8 on Dobbin to win at 6/1'. Alternatively, you can say '48 to 8 Dobbin'.

When you place a bet you will be given a ticket with the bookmaker's name and a number on it. The ticket has no details about your selection or how much you have staked. All of those details appear in the bookmaker's ledger. It is therefore important that you listen to make sure that the bookmaker correctly repeats your bet, as the clerk will write down whatever he shouts out. If you think a mistake has been made, query it immediately. Pay particular attention if there are two or more horses with similar names in the same race. Also, make a note of the bet yourself. If you make several bets you may not remember all the details of each bet.

Be sure to place your bet in good time, as there is always a last-minute rush. If you leave it too late you may not get your bet on. You will only be able to collect your winnings from the bookmaker with whom you placed the bet, as they are all independent.

There are several advantages to betting with bookmakers at the racecourse. You get to see the horses in the paddock before they run. This gives you the opportunity to see the horse's condition at close quarters and to spot anything amiss that may affect its running.

You see the racing live. This means that if you see an incident that leads to a stewards' enquiry or objection or are well enough placed to judge which horse has won a photo finish, you can make some extra money by betting on the outcome. You also have more choice, as the prices that individual bookmakers offer will vary. You have the opportunity to shop around for the best price. A lot of betting takes place before prices are transmitted to betting shops so you are able to take advantage of earlier shows. You also have the chance to negotiate a better price with the bookmaker, as they are all independent. You are able to take a fixed price, so know exactly what you will win. You can also compare the prices on offer with the bookmakers with those on the tote.

There are some disadvantages, too. You have to pay for admission charges and for the cost of travelling. It is also time-consuming to go to a race meeting. You will need to decide for yourself whether or not it is cost effective to attend the meeting or whether you should simply go to a betting shop. The deciding factor will most likely be your level of stakes. If you intend to place large bets, you are likely to benefit from attending the meeting. If your bets will be small, any advantages in prices will tend to be outweighed by the admission and travelling costs.

Tote betting

Tote is short for totalizator, which is a betting system where the total of the bets on a race are divided among those betting on the winner. A deduction is made for tax, money returned to racing and running costs. The amount deducted varies from country to country.

This system is completely independent from bookmakers and any bets placed with bookmakers do not affect the winnings paid. Prices offered by bookmakers bear no relation to the prices paid on the tote.

At the racecourse you will see a large board showing the number of bets placed on each runner, the total value of the bets and the payouts. Alternatively, these details will be displayed on television screens. There are different figures for different types of bet. These figures are constantly changing as more money is bet. As soon as the race is off, betting stops.

If you have bet on a horse to win and it comes in first, you will have a share of the win pool. The amount you win will depend on how many other people also have selected the winner, much like a lottery. If you are the only person who has picked the winner then you will receive all the money in the win pool. If 500 people have bet on the winner, then you will receive 1/500 of the pool.

The highest recorded tote odds for a win bet were 3410¼/1. They were paid on a horse called Coole at British racecourse Haydock Park on 30 November 1929.

In Great Britain, the most common tote bets are:

- ▶ win: *the selection to win*
- ▶ place: *the number of places depends on the number of runners*
- ▶ each way: *a bet on the horse to win and a bet on the horse to be placed*
- ▶ exacta: *predicting the first and second in correct order*
- ▶ trifecta: *predicting which horses will be first, second and third in the correct order*
- ▶ quadpot: *predicting which horses will be placed in the four quadpot races (usually races 3 to 6)*
- ▶ jackpot: *predicting which horses will win in each race of a meeting (usually the first six races)*
- ▶ placepot: *predicting which horses will be placed in each race of a meeting (usually the first six races)*
- ▶ scoop 6: *selecting the winners in six nominated televised races*
- ▶ multibets, *like doubles trebles, accumulator, patent, yankee or super 15 can also be played.*

Dividends are quoted to a £1 stake.

For place bets, the number of places that count are as follows:

Number of runners	Places
1–4	Win only
5–7	First and second
8+	First, second and third
16+ handicaps	First, second, third and fourth

Pari-mutuel

Pari-mutuel is basically a system similar to tote betting with slightly different rules. The money on each selection is also pooled and divided between the winners after deductions. The main difference is the way that horses from the same stable are treated. If, for example, horses A and B from the same stable are running, they are coupled. This means that a bet for horse A to win is also a bet for horse B to win. If you place a bet on horse A to win, you will also win if horse B wins the race. The coupling only applies to win bets and not to place, show or exotic bets.

Pari-mutuel betting is found in the United States and continental Europe.

In the United States, the most common bets are:

- ▶ win: *the selection to win*
- ▶ place: *the selection must finish first or second*
- ▶ show: *the selection must finish first, second or third*
- ▶ exacta/perfecta: *predicting first and second in the correct order*
- ▶ trifecta: *predicting first, second and third in the correct order*
- ▶ daily double: *predicting the winners in the first two races of the day.*

Bets other than win, place and show are called exotics.

Dividends are quoted to a $2 stake.

Bookmaking

HOW PRICES ARE DETERMINED

A bookmaker uses an expert called a handicapper to assess
the chances of each runner in the race. The handicapper will
consider a number of factors to determine the chances of each
horse. Things like pedigree, recent performance, the jockey,
weight carried and the condition of the ground will be taken
into account. A book of prices is then made depending on the
assessment. The runner that he thinks is most likely to win will
have the lowest price and is called the favourite. Occasionally
two runners are deemed to have an equal chance of winning.
They will have the same price and be called joint favourites.
If several runners have the same lowest price they are called
co-favourites.

The prices of the horses in a race can vary enormously. Just
because a horse has a large price it does not mean that it will
not win. In 1990 Equinoctial won at Kelso at a price of 250/1 –
the longest odds recorded in British horse racing.

The initial prices offered are called tissue prices. This is just
a preliminary indication of the prices and they tend to be a
conservative estimate of a horse's chance of winning. Once bets
have been made the prices are said to have been laid. This means
a betting market has been made. The prices then change depending
on how much money is bet. The prices do not show the chances
that a horse has of winning. Instead, they reflect how much money
has been bet on them. The horse attracting the greatest amount
of money in bets will have the lowest price. The horse attracting

the least amount of money will have the highest price. Horses with high prices are called outsiders or rags.

Insight

The prices quoted on a horse race will constantly change depending on how much money is bet on them. The price of a horse can drastically change between its tissue price and its starting price.

BAR

When prices are quoted for a race, the odds for some outsiders may not be given. Instead, a bar price is shown. This means that all the horses not quoted in the betting are at a higher price than that given in the bar. For example in a ten-runner race, prices may be given for seven of the runners and a bar price of 25/1. This means that the other three horses all have a price of greater than 25/1. If you want to place a bet on one of the unquoted horses, you will need to agree a price with the bookmaker.

Understanding the odds

Crucial to betting on horse racing is an understanding of the odds or prices. The odds or prices give an indication of your potential winnings and whether or not making a bet is worthwhile.

There is a huge variety of different types of odds and prices. There are also a lot of slang expressions used to describe the odds. Sometimes you may take a price but certain conditions may mean that this price is altered. The occurrence of dead heats, withdrawn horses and joint favourites may mean you are paid out less than you expected.

When you go to place a bet, you will see that there are prices (odds) quoted for the runners. These prices are usually made up of two numbers with a slash between, for example 5/4, 11/8, 5/1,

7/2, 15/2, 25/1. These prices are a ratio telling you what you will win for a particular stake. The amount on the left of the price is what you will win if you bet the amount on the right. The money bet is called the stake. If you win, your stake is refunded. The total amount won is called the returns or payout.

Examples

If the price quoted is 6/1, you will win £6 for every £1 staked. Your stake is also refunded. If you bet £5 on a horse at 6/1, your returns will be (6 x 5) + 5 = £35.

If you bet £4 on a horse at odds of 6/4, your returns will be 6 + 4 = £10.

If you bet £1 on a horse at odds of 11/2 your returns will be 5.5 + 1 = £6.50.

ODDS AGAINST AND ODDS ON

Where the number on the left of the price is bigger than the number on the right the term odds against is used; where it is less it is called odds on. Where both numbers are the same, i.e. 1/1, the term even money or evens is used.

Examples

1/1 is even money (always written as 'evens').

13/8 is odds against, 8/13 is odds on.

5/2 is odds against, 2/5 is odds on.

You will often hear prices quoted with the word 'on', for example, '2/1 on'. This actually means that the price is 1/2. Therefore when the word 'on' is quoted, to find the correct price the order of the price needs to be reversed: '11/8 on' is 8/11, '7/4 on' is 4/7 and '6/5 on' is 5/6. This can lead to confusion, particularly if you mishear. When prices are announced in betting shops they are given in the correct order.

EACH WAY

Bookmakers also accept each-way bets. This is two bets. One bet is for the horse to win the race and the other is for it to be placed second, third or fourth. The number of places paid depends on the number of runners in the race (see the table on page 29). It is important to pay particular attention to the number of places paid as some bookmakers offer lower odds than others.

Insight

Suppose there are four places paid in a race. The returns on the place bet of an each-way bet will be the same regardless of whether your horse came in first, second, third or fourth.

Example

Suppose you bet £10 each way on a horse. Your stake will be £20 because an each-way bet is two bets. If the horse wins at 4/1 and 1/4 of the odds are paid for the place:

The win part of the bet pays (4 x 10) + 10 = £50.

The place part of the bet pays only 1/4 the odds of the win. To find the correct odds to calculate the returns you need to multiply the number on the right of the price by 4. (If the bet was at 1/5 odds you would need to multiply by 5.)

(Contd)

So the win odds of 4/1 become place odds of 4/4 (which is evens – 1/1). So the place part pays (1 x 10) + 10 = £20.

The total returns are £50 + £20 = £70.

If your horse wins the race, one bet will be settled at the full odds but the other bet will be settled at a fraction of the odds.

If the horse were to come second, the win bet would be lost but the place bet would be won. The returns would be £20.

In races where there are four runners or fewer, it is not possible to bet each way. It is only possible to bet on the winner. If an each-way bet is placed, all the stakes go on the horse to win. This is called all up and is often abbreviated to au.

For place bets the number of places that count are as shown in the table on page 29.

TIC-TAC

The bookmakers at the racecourse use a system of hand signals called tic-tac to communicate prices and bets made to one another. At the racecourse you will hear a lot of slang used for the prices.

jolly: favourite
evens: levels
11/10 tips
5/4 wrist
11/8 up the arm
6/4 ear 'ole
7/4 shoulder

15/8 *double tops*
2/1 *bottle*
5/2 *face*
11/4 *elef a vier*
3/1 *carpet*
100/30 *burlington bertie*
4/1 *rouf*
5/1 *hand*
9/2 *on the shoulders*
6/1 *exes*
7/1 *neves*
9/1 *enin*
10/1 *cockle*
11/1 *elef*
12/1 *net and bice*
14/1 *net and rouf*
16/1 *net and ex*
20/1 *double net*
25/1 *macaroni*
25/1 *pony*
33/1 *double carpet*
100/1 *century*

Once a bookmaker has decided what his initial prices are, he will offer them to the punters. As money is bet, the bookmaker calculates his liability should that selection win. If the book does not balance with the prices currently on offer, he will adjust the prices accordingly.

When a bet is placed the bookmaker will call out the winnings to the stake that has been bet and give a ticket to the punter. There are no details of the bet marked on the ticket. Instead, it is just marked with a number that corresponds to an entry in the bookmaker's ledger. The bookmaker's clerk will enter the bet into the ledger. The ledger will have a section for each runner. The details that are kept are the stakes and winnings on each bet, the cumulative stakes and winnings and the punters ticket number. A running total of the stakes is also kept.

By comparing the cumulative stake with the total stakes, the bookmaker can easily see what his liabilities are. If any of the cumulative stake figures exceed the total stakes, then the prices on those runners need to be reduced. The runners where the liabilities are less than the total stakes can have their prices lengthened.

Example

If we look at two of the runners in a race, the prices on offer may be as follows: runner A 1/4; runner B 2/1.

Suppose the following bets were made:

1 £40 win A
2 £20 win B
3 £20 win A
4 £5 win B

By comparing the total stake to the cumulative winnings on each runner, the liability can be calculated.

Bookmaker's ledger for recording bets

Selection A

a	b	c	d	e
50	10	40	40	1
75	5	20	60	3

Selection B

a	b	c	d	e
60	40	20	20	2
75	10	5	25	4

a = cumulative returns
b = returns
c = stake
d = cumulative stake
e = ticket number

	Total stake	If A wins	If B wins
1	40	lose £10	win £40
2	60	win £10	break even
3	80	win £5	break even
4	85	win £10	break even

At this stage, the bookmaker may decide to shorten the price on B in order to increase his profit.

ARE YOU BEING OFFERED A GOOD PRICE?

When you assess your horse, make an estimate about what price it should be in the betting. How does your estimate compare to its actual price? Are you getting value for money?

Factors affecting prices

Even though you may have taken a price, the odds at which your bet is settled may be adjusted if certain conditions apply.

NON-RUNNERS

A non-runner is a horse that does not take part in the race. A horse may be withdrawn any time up to the off. If you bet on a non-runner on the day of the race, your stake will be refunded. If, however, you bet ante-post, you will lose your stake.

If a horse comes under starter's orders in a race but refuses to run, it is not considered a non-runner. It is important to check the results because a horse can be withdrawn right up to the last minute. You may see it set off for the start, but it may, for example, be withdrawn because it refuses to go into the starting stalls.

WITHDRAWN HORSES

Rule 4 deductions
After a book has been made on a race, a horse may be withdrawn. This will mean that the prices offered on the race will be incorrect, as they would have been worked out including the withdrawn horse. The bookmakers are therefore allowed to make an adjustment to the prices, called a rule 4 deduction (usually abbreviated to R4). The deduction is quoted as an amount in the pound, for example 10p in the £. The amount of the deduction is determined by the price of the withdrawn horse (see table). The deduction applies to both winning and placed horses. Only the winnings are affected and not your stake.

Insight
A rule 4 deduction is a means for bookmakers to balance their books when a horse has been taken out of the betting. A rule 4 of 50p in the £ will mean that your winnings will be reduced by 50%.

Rule 4 deductions

Odds of horse withdrawn		Deduction	% of winnings
3/10 or shorter		75p in £	75
Over 3/10	up to and including 2/5	70p in £	70
Over 2/5	up to and including 8/15	65p in £	65
Over 8/15	up to and including 8/13	60p in £	60
Over 8/13	up to and including 4/5	55p in £	55

Over 4/5	up to and including 20/21	50p in £	50
Over 20/21	up to and including 6/5	45p in £	45
Over 6/5	up to and including 6/4	40p in £	40
Over 6/4	up to and including 7/4	35p in £	35
Over 7/4	up to and including 9/4	30p in £	30
Over 9/4	up to and including 3/1	25p in £	25
Over 3/1	up to and including 4/1	20p in £	20
Over 4/1	up to and including 11/2	15p in £	15
Over 11/2	up to and including 9/1	10p in £	10
Over 9/1	up to and including 14/1	5p in £	5
Over 14/1		no deduction	

Insight

If you have a bet on a withdrawn horse, it is treated as a non-runner. This means for a bet placed on the day of the race that your stake will be refunded. If you bet ante-post you will lose your stake.

Example

A horse that was 4/1 in the betting is withdrawn. The SP of the winning horse is 2/1. The price will be subject to a rule 4 deduction of 20p in the £.

A £10 bet tax paid on a winning horse at 2/1 would normally return £30. With a rule 4 deduction of 20p in the £, the bet would return £26.

Calculation: (20 – 20%) + 10 = 26.

If there is sufficient time before the race is off, a new book will be made. In this case, the rule 4 deduction will apply to prices taken before the time that the new book was made. Prices taken on the new book and SP prices will not be subject to a rule 4 deduction.

Each-way bets

Horses being withdrawn can also affect the odds paid and the number of places paid for each-way bets. When you placed your bet there may have been eight runners, meaning you would expect to be paid if your horse came third. However, if a horse is withdrawn, the third placed horse no longer counts, as there will only be seven runners. You will only be paid if your horse is first or second.

Dead heats

Occasionally, two horses or more are declared the winner. This is a dead heat. When a horse dead heats for first place, the returns are halved. If there are three horses in the dead heat, then the returns are divided by three. If placed horses dead heat, the returns are only reduced if there are more places that usual being paid. For example, if two horses dead heat for second place and three places would normally be paid, the returns will not be affected. If, however, only two places would normally be paid and two horses dead heat for second place, the returns of the placed horses will be affected. So too will the returns of any each-way bets on the winner.

Insight

Suppose a horse dead-heats for second place and there are just three places being paid out. The horse that comes in third will not count as being placed.

Placing a tote bet

At the racecourse, you simply go to the tote or pari-mutuel counter and tell the member of staff the number of the horse you have selected, the type of bet you want and how much you want to stake. For bets that involve more than one race, like placepot and jackpot you will usually be required to fill in a betting slip. At some racecourses, machines have been installed for issuing tickets.

You will be presented with a printed ticket. Always check that it is marked with the correct details. Keep your ticket in a safe place, as you will need it to collect your winnings. Don't throw it away until after the weigh-in is announced. Even if your horse finished last there could still be a stewards' enquiry, which could lead to an amended result or even to a race being declared void. If a race is declared void, you will be entitled to claim your stake back. To collect your winnings, simply present your ticket at the payout window.

The rules vary depending on where you bet. For some forecast bets the selections must finish in the correct order; for others the order is not important. You should carefully read the rules and make sure you understand them before you bet.

The advantage of betting on the tote is that you can bet for small stakes. It can be more profitable to back outsiders on the tote as close to the off their odds are not always lengthened by bookmakers.

The main disadvantage with betting on the tote is that you are betting blind, as you do not know in advance what your winnings will be. When you bet with a bookmaker, you can take the price on offer, so therefore you can work out exactly how much you will win. With the tote you get a rough guide of what the dividends will pay. This is constantly changing and is updated as more bets are placed. The dividend may change hugely between when you put your bet on and when the race is declared off. There may be a flurry of betting with the bookmakers, which drastically lowers the price of a horse. This may prompt those betting on the tote to also back this horse, which will drive down the dividend for that particular horse. It is not until after the race that you will know exactly how much the dividends will pay.

10 THINGS TO REMEMBER

1 *Bookmaking is a system of betting on fixed odds or prices.*

2 *When betting with on-course bookmakers listen carefully to the bet that is called out.*

3 *The Tote is a betting system where the total bets made are divided between those betting on the winner.*

4 *Tote prices bear no relation to bookmaker's prices.*

5 *With Pari-mutuel bets, horses from the same stable are coupled.*

6 *Evens is a price of 1/1.*

7 *Bookmakers prices are a ratio of winnings to stake.*

8 *An each-way bet is two bets, one bet for the horse to win and one bet for it to be placed.*

9 *The price may be affected by a non-runner or a dead heat.*

10 *Don't throw away betting slips straight away – there may be a stewards' enquiry which could change the result.*

3

Betting shops

In this chapter you will learn:
- **about types of price**
- **the disadvantages of using a betting shop**
- **about types of bet.**

Fixed-odds betting shops, often called bookies, operate in countries including Great Britain and Ireland. In Great Britain, there are licensed betting shops. There are major chains of betting shops run by large companies and lots of independent operators. Betting shops offer a wide variety of different types of prices and bets. They operate in a similar way to bookmakers by offering prices at fixed odds. Some of their prices are determined by what the on-course bookmakers are offering. Other prices are decided by the betting shops themselves. Some are only available at certain times.

In recent years there has been much deregulation, which has allowed extended opening hours to cover evening and Sunday racing. They offer a wide range of facilities including:

- *betting on virtually any sporting event*
- *a wide range of different bets*
- *live transmission of horse racing, greyhound racing and other sporting events*
- *amusement machines*
- *refreshments*

- *telephone betting*
- *credit and deposit accounts.*

The pages of the major sporting newspapers are arranged around the walls. They give the day's race card, form and tips. Television screens display lots of information, including the latest prices and the previous day's results. Pens are provided for the filling in of betting slips. The betting shop staff stand behind a counter and process bets and pay out winnings.

Types of price

ANTE-POST PRICES

When a bet is placed before the day of the event it is called an ante-post bet. For major races like the Grand National and the Derby, prices are available many months before they are run. The prices are normally more favourable than those offered on the day of the event. However, if your runner is withdrawn from the race, your stake is automatically lost.

Sometimes, too many horses are entered for a race. For safety reasons, only a certain number may run. In this situation, a procedure called balloting out will determine which horses run. If your runner is balloted out, your stakes will be refunded. The prices of the remaining horses will be adjusted according to rule 4 (see pages 38–39).

Although ante-post betting has its risks, such as horses being withdrawn, the benefit of the higher prices is usually advantageous to the punter.

EARLY MORNING PRICES

Most betting shops offer prices on several races as soon as they open for business. These are usually on the handicap races but some may give prices on all the races. These prices are quite often advertised in the sporting press. It is worthwhile comparing the prices offered by different operators, as they will vary.

As soon as betting starts on the race prices will change. Some betting shops will allow customers to take the advertised price up to a certain amount of time after the shop is open. Some also guarantee that if their early morning prices are worse than the starting prices, the bet will be settled at the starting price. If you want to take the early morning prices you should place your bet as early as possible. The prices will only be available up to the first show (see next section).

The races will be running the same day, so if your selection does not run, your stake will be refunded.

BOARD PRICES/SHOWS

Around ten minutes before the race starts prices will be passed from the racecourse. The prices represent an average of what bookmakers on the course are offering. Once the betting shop has received these prices, early morning prices can no longer be taken. Board prices will change continually as money is bet on the runners up to the start of the race. Each new set of prices that is transmitted is called a show. The first set of prices transmitted is called the first show. The name board prices comes from the old custom of writing the prices on a board in the betting shop. Nowadays, the prices appear on television screens. As well as the current price on offer, the previous shows are also given. The current price is the one that is furthest to the right. As the start of the race approaches, prices change with greater frequency.

STARTING PRICES

Usually abbreviated to SP, the starting prices are an average of the prices that a sample of on-course bookmakers are offering at the start of the race, as agreed by the starting price executive. The starting price executive is made up of three major media companies, the Press Association, Trinity Mirror and Satellite Information Services. They employ starting price returners who make a note of prices offered in the betting ring for all horses in each race, just before the off. An average of these prices is used to calculate the starting price.

When the results of the races are published in the press, the starting prices will be quoted. If you have taken a price like an early price or ante-post price, then your bet will be settled at the odds taken, regardless of the starting price. If you do not take any of the prices previously mentioned, then your bet will be settled at the starting price. In the event that no prices are quoted, the bets will be settled using the tote dividends.

TOTE DIVIDENDS

Tote dividends are quoted by the official tote on the racecourse. Most bookmakers take bets on the tote and will have a sign stating that they are authorized to take them. For bets at tote odds there are dividends quoted to a £1 stake for win, place, forecast, tricast, placepots and jackpots.

When placing a tote bet with a betting shop it is important to clearly mark 'TOTE' on the betting slip. Failure to do so will result in the bet being settled at starting price.

When you place a tote bet in a betting shop your money does not go into the pool. The betting shop simply allows you the convenience of betting on the prices that will be attained by these markets.

If you place a tote bet, you have no idea what is currently in the pools at the racecourse.

The dividends returned can vary quite considerably from the starting prices. This tends to happen more frequently at minor race meetings where the betting market is not strong. The problem with placing a tote bet in a betting shop is that you do not get the full benefit if the tote returns are much better than the starting prices. Most betting shops place a limit on how much they will pay on the tote, relative to the starting price. The maximum can be as much as four times the starting price equivalent but may be much lower. However, you will often be guaranteed a minimum payout; a minimum of half the starting price equivalent is common.

Large tote bets placed in betting shops are subject to scrutiny as they are often used in betting coups. At a race meeting with a poor attendance, the betting market can be weak. This makes it easier to manipulate. Suppose you want to back a horse. If you bet at the track, your bet goes into the tote and reduces the dividend for that horse. Relatively small bets can completely alter the dividends and return an artificially high dividend on one horse. If this horse is backed with tote bets in a betting shop, these bets do not affect the eventual tote dividend. If the horse wins, the dividend is artificially high.

FORECAST AND TRICAST

These are quoted to a £1 stake from the racecourse. Sometimes bookmakers may offer their own forecast prices, most commonly for overseas racing, where a dividend may not be given from the racecourse.

BETTING ON FOREIGN RACING

With the innovation of satellite transmission of racing, it is becoming more common for coverage to be given for major overseas racing. Simulcasting allows betters in another country to bet directly into the pools at a foreign racecourse. An example of this is betting on the Breeders' Cup and the Prix de l'Arc de Triomphe, which allow British betters to bet on the tote at the racecourse.

If you bet in British betting shops on French racing you have the choice of betting on the pari-mutuel (French tote) or with the betting shop's prices. It is not possible to predict what is better, but at least if you take a price you know in advance what your winnings will be.

PARI-MUTUEL DIVIDENDS

Pari-mutuel is the name of the French horse racing tote. The dividends are quoted to a €1 stake.

One major difference with the French system of betting is the coupling of horses. If horses from the same stable are running in the same race, then the same price for those horses will be given in the betting. The horses are said to be coupled. A bet on one horse from that stable is also a bet on any one of the other horses from the same stable. Therefore, if horses A and B are coupled and a £1 win is placed on horse A, the bet will also hold if horse B wins.

If, however, you take the betting shop's price on a horse, your horses will not be coupled.

Insight: Prices given in newspapers

When a newspaper prints the race cards, they will usually quote prices for the runners. These are a guide only as to what the particular newspaper expects the starting prices to be. They will vary from paper to paper. It is not possible to take these prices.

Disadvantages of using a betting shop

LATE TRANSMISSION OF PRICES

A major problem with using betting shops is the lateness of the transmission of the prices from the racecourse. At the racecourse, betting on the next race starts as soon as the previous race has finished. However, prices are not transmitted to the betting shops until around 15 minutes before the race, sometimes later. This delay can mean that you have missed out on more favourable prices. Big changes could have taken place in the prices, none of which you can see. The betting shops argue that they are waiting for a market to be formed and that they are not conning you out of money. However, had you been at the racecourse, you would have had the opportunity to bet sooner.

As the off time of the race nears, betting on the lower priced runners becomes more frantic, because, as more money pours onto them, their odds get shorter. The prices of the outsiders should become correspondingly bigger; however, in practice, they often don't. There simply isn't time. On the course you can negotiate a price with the bookmaker, as he is independent. With the off-course bookmakers it is not possible to negotiate. The result is that the off-course bookmaker's profit increases.

Writing a bet

Some betting shops have introduced machines for placing bets, however, in the vast majority of shops you need to write your bet onto a betting slip.

Most bets are written on plain two-piece betting slips. You write on the top sheet and the bottom sheet is carbonized so it automatically makes a copy.

Some bets are written on special slips. These are common bets like lucky 15s, alphabets, union jack and tricast. Some bookmakers insist that a bet must be written on a certain type of slip to qualify for bonuses or consolations. It is therefore worth checking if the bet that you are making comes into this category.

Print everything in capital letters as the settler will need to be able to read what you have written, so the clearer the better. If he can't read it, he can't settle it.

If you are making several bets, do not cram them all onto one slip. Use a separate slip for each. This not only makes settling your bet easier, it also makes is simpler for you to check that your bets are correctly staked.

The details you need to give on the bet are:

▶ *name or race card number of your selection*
▶ *off time of the race*
▶ *name of the meeting*

▶ *your stake*
▶ *the type of bet.*

Example bet

Ascot 2.30	meeting and time
Dobbin	name of selection
£1 win	instructions for the bet
Stake £1.00	stake
Total stake = £1.00	total stake

TIME AND MEETING

It is important to include the time and meeting if you want your bet settled quickly. This applies even if you are betting on the next race. In busy betting shops where the settler has lots of bets to settle, untimed bets will usually be put to the bottom of the pile and dealt with after all the timed bets have been settled.

Forgetting to put the time of the race on your bet can cause problems if, instead of naming the horse, you just identify it by its race card number. You may intend betting on, for example, number 6 in the next horse race. However, if you do not time the bet and a greyhound race is run immediately after you place the bet, it will be settled on the result of the greyhound race.

Although it is more time consuming, it is better to always write the horse's name to avoid this problem. Extra care should also be taken if there are two horses running with similar names.

MISTAKES ON BETTING SLIPS

It cannot be stressed enough that you should carefully check everything that you have written on your bet. Mistakes are all too common. The settler can only act on what you have written on the slip and not on what you meant to write. The person who takes your bet is not responsible for checking it. They simply do not have the time to read every single bet that is placed. If you have any problems with a bet, the person to speak to is the shop manager. Any errors will be settled in accordance with the shop's rules.

PLACING A BET

Your completed slip should be handed to the cashier with the necessary money. The bet will not be processed until the money has been handed to the cashier.

You can pay with either cash or cheque. Credit cards are not acceptable. If you want to pay by cheque, you should inform the cashier at least 15 minutes before the start of the race, so that the cheque can be processed. If left any later the bet may be refused.

You have the option of either taking the price on offer at the time the bet is placed or having the bet settled at starting price or tote odds. If you wish to take the current price on offer you should tell the cashier when you place your bet. The cashier will then mark the bet with the price and initial it. It is not acceptable to simply write the price on yourself and say nothing.

When a race is declared off, the cashier will process a slip through the till. Any bets taken after this 'off slip' will be void, win or lose. Try to get your bets on early because there is always a last-minute rush, particularly on busy race days like Grand National day.

You can avoid the queues by betting early in the morning or even placing your bets the day before. Due to the huge number of bets placed on busy race days it can take some time before winnings can be collected. Unless you are desperate for your money (or enjoy queuing) it is better to collect your winnings during the following week.

WHAT HAPPENS IF YOU LOSE YOUR BETTING SLIP?

Unlike betting at the racecourse, there is no problem if you lose your betting slip. Because the bets are handwritten and everyone's

handwriting is unique, your bet can soon be identified if you write
out a copy of it. You will usually be required to fill in a form
to claim the winnings. Small amounts will be paid out directly.
For larger amounts you may have to produce some form of
identification, such as a driver's licence.

Bookmakers' rules

All bookmakers have a set of rules displayed in their shop. These
cover such things as maximum payouts, what happens if an error
is made on a bet and conditions that may apply to certain bets.
The rules vary in different chains of shops, so if you are betting in
a different shop then it is worth checking if the same conditions
apply. Unfortunately, the rules tend to be full of jargon and not
written in plain English. If you have any trouble interpreting them,
the shop manager is the best person to ask.

UNNAMED FAVOURITES

The favourite is the runner with the lowest price. It is possible to bet
on the favourite without actually naming it. However, it is possible
for more than one runner to be the favourite. If two runners have
the same lowest price they are called joint favourites. Should there be
several runners with the lowest prices, they are called co-favourites.
Should an unnamed favourite win (i.e. you have just written the
favourite to win on your betting slip), the returns will be divided
by however many favourites there are. Since prices can change very
quickly, the prices can differ hugely between when you first place
your bet and when the starting prices are returned. If you intend to
bet on a particular horse, it is much better to name it on your slip.

PAYOUT EXCEEDS BOOKMAKER'S LIMIT

Bookmakers place limits on how much they will pay out. For the
larger chains of bookmakers the limits are high. However, small
bookmakers have much lower limits. Before you place a large bet,

you should check that your potential payout does not exceed this limit. It is worthless placing for example a £100 bet, if a £50 bet is sufficient to reach the payout limit.

WEIGH-IN

After a race the winning and placed jockeys have to weigh in to make sure that any weight they were carrying is correct. Most betting shops pay out winning bets, up to a certain amount, before the weigh-in. If a stewards' enquiry is announced, the result of the race may be amended. If you have collected your winnings and your horse is subsequently disqualified, you are not obliged to return the money to the bookmaker. If your horse was placed and is made the winner, the difference between what you have collected so far and what you are entitled to will be paid.

For betting purposes, once the weigh-in has been announced the result will stand regardless of subsequent events. Only very rarely will a result be amended after the weigh-in. This is usually if a horse has been positively tested for drugs. So if you are unfortunate enough to bet on the horse that came second, you will not be paid out as a winner.

OBJECTIONS AND STEWARDS' ENQUIRIES

If an objection or a stewards' enquiry is called, the bookmaker will stop paying out on that race. The stewards will then look at the race and decide whether or not any rules have been broken. If the rules have been breached then the stewards may amend the result by disqualifying runners, altering the order of the placed horses, or voiding the race. It is therefore important not to throw away your betting slip until the runners have officially weighed in.

DEPOSIT/CREDIT ACCOUNTS

Most betting shops offer this service. It allows you to place bets over the telephone. Calls are recorded to minimize disputes. Deposit accounts allow you to deposit a certain amount of money with the betting shop and to place bets over the telephone up to the balance of your account. With credit accounts you are granted a certain amount of credit, which will depend on your financial circumstances. The main disadvantage with this method of betting is that the minimum stakes are higher than those in betting shops.

Types of bet

Betting shops offer a wide variety of bets. These are some of the most common.

WIN SINGLE

One bet on the winner of a race.

EACH-WAY SINGLE

Two bets, one bet for the selection to win and the other for it to be placed. The place bet is settled as a fraction of the win odds. The number of places and the fraction of odds vary depending on how many runners there are and the type of race as shown in the table.

....

Insight

If you back a horse each-way and it wins a handicap race with 14 runners, the win stake will be paid at full odds and the place stake at 1/4 odds. If however your horse came third, the win stake would be lost but the place stake would be paid at 1/4 odds.

Suppose you bet each-way on a race with just three runners and your horse wins, the win bet will be paid at full odds and the place bet will also be paid at full odds.

If you bet each-way on a non-handicap race and your horse comes fourth, both bets will lose. The win part of the bet will lose as your horse does not win the race and the place part loses as only the first three places count in this type of race.

....

Number of places and fraction of odds paid for the place bet, determined by number of runners and type of race

Number of runners	Type of race	Number of places	Fraction of win odds
16 or more	handicap	4	1/4
12 to 15	handicap	3	1/4
8 to 15	not applicable	3	1/5
5 to 7	not applicable	2	1/4
4 or less	not applicable	1 (win only)	both bets win

DOUBLE

A win double is one bet on two runners to win two different races. If the first selection wins, the returns are put on to the second selection.

An each-way double is two separate bets of a win double and a place double on two runners in two different races. The win bet is the same as a win double. For the place part of the bet, if the first selection is placed the returns become the stake for the second selection to be placed.

TREBLE

One bet on three selections in three different races. If the first selection wins, the returns are put on to the second selection and if the second selection wins the returns are put onto the third selection.

ACCUMULATOR

A bet on any number of selections, in different races, where the winnings on the first horse go onto the second and then onto the third and then onto the fourth and so on. It is one bet win and two bets each way. Obviously, the returns can be quite large, depending on the prices of the winning selections. It is therefore worth checking that your winnings would not exceed the bookmaker's maximum payout.

STRAIGHT FORECAST

Nominating which selections will finish first and second in the correct order.

REVERSED FORECAST

Nominating two selections to finish first and second in either order. It is two bets.

COMBINATION/FULL COVER FORECAST

Selecting any number of runners in one race to finish first and second in either order. To calculate how may bets there are, simply multiply the number of selections by one number less:

3 selections is 3 × 2 = 6 bets
4 selections is 4 × 3 = 12 bets
5 selections is 5 × 4 = 20 bets.

WITH THE FIELD FORECAST/AGAINST THE FIELD FORECAST

A forecast where the winner is nominated and any of the other runners in the race can be second. For example, if you select Dobbin to win you would write on the betting slip 'Dobbin to win against the field', or 'Dobbin to win with the field'.

Alternatively, a selection can be nominated to finish second and for any of the other runners to win. This bet would be written as 'Dobbin to finish second against the field', or 'Dobbin to finish second with the field'.

To calculate the number of bets in both cases deduct one from the number of runners in the race. For a race with eight runners it is seven bets. For a race with ten runners it is nine bets.

TRICAST

Selecting three runners in the same race to finish first, second and third in the correct order.

TRIXIE

Three selections in three different races, comprising three doubles and one treble. It is four bets win and eight bets each way.

YANKEE

Four selections in four different races, comprising six doubles, four trebles and one fourfold. It is 11 bets win and 22 bets each way.

MIX

Similar to a yankee, except there are double the stakes on the fourfold. Four selections in four different races, comprising six doubles, four trebles and a double-staked fourfold. It is 11 bets but, as the fourfold is double-staked the unit stake should be multiplied by 12 for win bets and 24 for each-way bets.

SUPER YANKEE/CANADIAN

Five selections in five different races, comprising ten doubles, ten trebles, five fourfolds and one fivefold. It is 26 bets win and 52 bets each way.

HEINZ

Six selections in six different races comprising 15 doubles, 20 trebles, 15 fourfolds, six fivefolds and one sixfold. It is 57 bets win and 114 bets each way.

SUPER HEINZ

Seven selections in seven different races, comprising 21 doubles, 35 trebles, 35 fourfolds, 21 fivefolds, seven sixfolds and one sevenfold. It is 120 bets win and 240 bets each way.

GOLIATH

Eight selections in eight different races, comprising 28 doubles, 56 trebles, 70 fourfolds, 56 fivefolds, 28 sixfolds, eight sevenfolds and one eightfold. It is 247 bets win and 494 bets each way.

PATENT/TWIST

Three selections in three different races, comprising three singles, three doubles and one treble. There are seven bets win and 14 bets each way.

PERM PATENT 4

Four selections in four different races, comprising an individual patent on each group of three selections. It is 28 bets win and 56 bets each way.

LUCKY 15

Four selections in four different races, comprising four singles, six doubles, four trebles and one fourfold. It is 15 bets win and 30 bets each way. If there are four winners a 10 per cent bonus is paid, usually at starting price. If there is only one winner, double the starting price odds are paid. These bonuses and consolations apply only to the win part of the bet. So if an each-way lucky 15 has just one placed horse, double the odds is not paid on the placed selection. Similarly, if one selection wins and one is a non-runner, the consolation is not paid.

LUCKY 31

Five selections in five different races, comprising five singles, ten doubles, ten trebles, five fourfolds and one fivefold. It is 31 bets win and 62 bets each way.

Bonuses paid vary with different bookmakers. Some pay a bonus on four winners and five winners, others pay a bonus on only five winners. It is certainly worth shopping around to find the best offers. A consolation of double the starting price odds is paid for one winner.

LUCKY 63

Six selections in six different races, comprising six singles, 15 doubles, 20 trebles, 15 fourfolds, six fivefolds and one sixfold. It is 63 bets win and 126 bets each way.

Bonuses vary with different bookmakers. A 10 per cent bonus is usually paid for five winners. For six winners the bonus is likely to be between 15 and 25 per cent. A consolation of double starting price odds is paid for one winner.

ANY TO COME

Two selections in two different races (although more can be played). If the first selection wins, a stake equal to the original stake is placed on the second selection. It is also possible to specify an amount of stake for the second bet.

SINGLE STAKES ABOUT/UP AND DOWN BET

Two selections in two different races. If the first selection wins, an amount equal to the original stake is put on the second selection and vice versa. It is two bets.

DOUBLE STAKES ABOUT/DOUBLE STAKES UP AND DOWN

As with the single stakes bet, except double the original stake is placed on the second selection and vice versa.

ROUNDER

Three selections in three different races, in three bets win and six bets each way. For selections A, B and C in a £1 rounder, the bets are as follows:

> *£1 win A any to come £1 win double on the other two selections.*
> *£1 win B any to come £1 win double on the other two selections.*
> *£1 win C any to come £1 win double on the other two selections.*

ROUNDABOUT

Three selections in three different races, in three bets. It is similar to a rounder, except double the original stakes are placed on the double.

For selections A, B and C in a £1 roundabout, the bets are as follows:

> *£1 win A any to come £2 win double BC.*
> *£1 win B any to come £2 win double AC.*
> *£1 win C any to come £2 win double AB.*

ROUND THE CLOCK

Any number of selections over three, in different races. It is one stake on the first selection any to come, one stake on the next selection, any to come, one stake on the next selection. This continues on each selection. For three selections it is three bets, or four selections it is four bets and so on.

For selections A, B and C in a 10p win round the clock, the stake is 30p. The bets are as follows:

> *10p win A any to come 10p win B any to come 10p win C.*
> *10p win B any to come 10p win C any to come 10p win A.*
> *10p win C any to come 10p win A any to come 10p win B.*

ROUND ROBIN

Three selections in three different races, in three doubles, one treble and six single stakes about bets. It is ten bets win and 20 bets each way.

For selections A, B and C the bets are as follows:

> *Doubles AB, AC, BC.*
> *Treble ABC.*
> *Single stakes about AB, AC, BC.*

FLAG

A bet on four selections in four different races, in a yankee and 12 single stakes about bets. It is 28 bets win and 56 bets each way.

SUPER FLAG

A bet that consists of a super yankee and ten single stakes about bets. It is 46 bets win and 92 bets each way.

Insight
Non-runners can be treated differently by some bookmakers. They may stipulate in their rules for multiple bets that a non-runner will be substituted for the favourite. It is therefore important to check the rules.

10 THINGS TO REMEMBER

1 *An ante-post price is a price quoted before the day of the race.*

2 *An early morning price is a price available as soon as the betting shop is open for business.*

3 *Board prices are an average of the prices that the on-course bookmakers are offering.*

4 *Tote dividends are the payouts made by the official tote on the racecourse.*

5 *When you write a bet, make sure you give all the details clearly – meeting, time, name of the horse, instructions for the bet and stake.*

6 *Check the bookmaker's rules.*

7 *Be aware of the implications of betting on an unnamed favourite.*

8 *Collect your winnings straight away.*

9 *Be aware that an objection or stewards' enquiry may affect the result.*

10 *You can still collect your winnings if you lose your betting slip.*

4

Remote betting

In this chapter you will learn:
- *about types of internet betting*
- *how to bet*
- *the advantages and disadvantages of internet betting*
- *how to play safe.*

Today's technology means that you no longer have to go to a racecourse or betting shop to place a bet. It is possible to place bets by a number of remote methods including via the internet, telephone and television. You will need to open an account with a betting firm and will be given details about how you can use the various methods. Some firms require you to deposit money with them before you can start betting. Others offer credit facilities.

Internet betting

WHAT IS INTERNET BETTING?

Internet betting, also referred to as online betting, is placing bets on horse racing via a computer connection over the internet. There are a number of ways to bet over the internet, including via bookmakers, betting exchanges and spread betting firms.

The internet betting firms supply computer software via their websites to allow you to place bets on horse racing all over the world, 24 hours a day, 7 days a week from the privacy of your own home.

IS INTERNET BETTING LEGAL?

In the UK, the Gambling Act 2005 legislates remote betting. Remote betting includes all types of betting where the parties involved in a bet are not face to face. This includes betting over the internet, telephone, via your television and future technology that may arise. The Gambling Act 2005 replaces most of the existing law about gambling in Great Britain. A new organization, the Gambling Commission, was formally established in autumn 2005 and is responsible for controlling gambling by regulating and licensing operators. Licensed gaming sites on the internet will carry a kitemark to show that the necessary standards have been met.

Betting exchanges come under the category of betting intermediaries and are required to have a betting intermediary operating licence from the Gambling Commission. They are required to keep customers' money in ring-fenced accounts.

Spread betting is classified in a different way. Due to its connection to trading on financial markets, all UK spread betting firms are regulated by the Financial Services Authority (FSA), an independent watchdog set up by government under the Financial Services and Markets Act 2000 to regulate financial services in the UK. The FSA has a firm check service, where you can find out if a firm is regulated and who to contact in the firm if you have an enquiry or complaint.

The FSA gives spread betting customers a certain degree of protection. If you have a complaint that you think has not been satisfactorily dealt with by the firm, you have access to the Financial Ombudsman Scheme. In addition, if a spread betting firm goes bust, you have access to the Financial Services

Compensation Scheme. The FSA website gives details about how to complain (see Taking it further on page 182).

In Australia, the Interactive Gambling Act 2001 prohibits online casino gambling but allows interactive sports betting and wagering services.

US federal law bans online gambling but online horse racing betting for operators authorized by American states is allowed.

HOW TO BET ON THE INTERNET

You will need a computer with an internet connection. Ideally, you should have a high-speed connection to keep up to date with rapidly changing prices and to ensure that your bets are speedily communicated to the betting firm's server. You will also need an account with an internet betting company. To get an account you will need to register with an internet betting firm and deposit money. The general requirements are that you are over 18 years of age and live in a place where internet betting is legal. Proof of your age and residence may be required. You will need to ensure that you comply with your own local, national or state laws before opening an account or placing a bet.

Registration involves selecting a user name and password which you will need to log on to the site. You should keep your password secret to stop other people logging on to your account and placing bets. You will need an email address so that you can be contacted by the internet company.

DEPOSITING AND WITHDRAWING MONEY

In order to start betting you will first need to deposit money with the internet betting company. Accounts are often available in a choice of currencies. Money can be deposited in various ways including credit cards, debit cards, cheques, money orders etc. For speed, credit cards and debit cards are ideal. They allow you to deposit funds directly and start betting immediately.

Types of internet betting

BOOKMAKERS

Betting opportunities are similar to those offered by on- and off-course bookmakers. Many of the UK high street bookmakers accept their range of bets over the internet and telephone. The range of bets available include single, multiple, each-way, forecast and tricast bets.

At the bookmaker's website you can find details of the race cards, prices, ratings, naps, form and statistics. Live commentaries of the races are given. The services are offered in a number of languages and bets can be made in a choice of currencies. Minimum stakes vary but can be as low as 1p. Maximum stakes and payouts vary from bookmaker to bookmaker so you should check the rules if you intend to make large bets. Many bookmakers also provide an online bet calculator so that you can easily work out your payout. Some bookmakers also give you the opportunity to see the odds as fractions or as decimals. This makes it easier to compare prices with betting exchanges (see next section). The bookmakers also provide price alerts that can be sent to you via email or mobile phone so that you can keep track of any changes.

Like a traditional bookmaker, there is a profit for the firm built into the prices of around 17 per cent.

BETTING EXCHANGES

What is a betting exchange?
Betting exchanges were introduced in 2000. Initially, concerns were raised about them affecting the integrity of racing due to them allowing bets on losing horses. These concerns have now been addressed with safeguards in place to monitor irregular patterns of betting. Due to the competitive prices offered, they have now become a popular way of betting.

A betting exchange acts as an agent to allow individuals to place bets with one another, charging a commission for its services. Suppose you wanted to have a bet with your friend on the favourite on the first race at Ascot. You think the horse will win and your friend thinks the horse will lose. You agree to stake £50 each and whoever wins takes the money staked. If your horse wins, you win the £100 and if your horse loses your friend wins the £100. In this situation, you have made a bet at 'evens' that your horse will win and your friend has made a bet at 'evens' that the horse will lose.

A betting exchange makes it possible for you to make bets like this with strangers. They provide the facilities to make the betting possible and charge a commission for their services. They provide a website that allows you to come into contact with other people who want to bet and the means to transfer money from one person to another. Both you and the other betters remain anonymous to each other. The betting exchange will keep details of the bets you have placed so that any foul play, such as people trying to manipulate the markets, can be investigated.

Insight

Using a betting exchange allows you to bet on a horse winning or losing. Back odds are prices for the horse to win. Lay odds are prices for the horse to lose.

Unlike a bookmaker, the betting exchange does not decide the prices of the horses, instead individuals making the bets do. In the previous example, each person had agreed to odds of evens. However, they could have decided to bet at different odds. Suppose your friend wanted to bet but was only willing to stake £25 and you were willing to bet £50. You would then be betting at odds of 1/2 that your horse would win and your friend would be betting at odds of 2/1 that the horse would lose. If the horse wins, you will win £75 less commission. If the horse loses, your friend will win £75 less commission. If you were placing the bet with a betting exchange you would basically indicate that you wanted to make a bet of 1/2 on the horse and therefore needed someone to make the opposite bet of 2/1. As soon as someone agrees to match your bet, it is made.

This arrangement gives greater flexibility than betting with a bookmaker. With a bookmaker, you can only bet on horses to win. With a betting exchange you can also bet that a horse will lose. With a traditional bookmaker, a horse may have a price of for example 4/1 and you can bet that the horse will win at 4/1. The bookmaker is effectively backing the horse to lose at 1/4. With a betting exchange you also have the opportunity to take the place of the bookmaker and bet that the horse will lose at 1/4.

Minimum stakes vary but are around £1–£2. Unlike with a bookmaker there is no maximum bet. As long as you can find someone to match your bet, you can stake as much as you wish.

Commission is charged at around 1–5 per cent. Different exchanges calculate the commission in different ways. Some charge commission on all bets placed (stakes) and others charge commission on net winnings. Some exchanges reduce the commission for loyal customers so that the more you bet the less the commission charged. Currently bets are tax free, however, this may change in the future as governments introduce legislation.

Insight

Commission rates vary with betting exchanges so it is worthwhile shopping around for the best deal. Make sure you understand how the commission is worked out before betting.

Advantages of using a betting exchange

The prices with a betting exchange are around 17 to 20 percent better than those offered by bookmakers. This is because bookmakers factor in a profit on every book that they make in order to cover their overheads and to make a profit. Since you are betting against an individual on a betting exchange, this does not apply. The prices will be determined by what other people are prepared to risk. Since they are only backing one horse, they do not have to make profit on all horses running like a bookmaker. You also have the advantage that you can ask for a better price than is currently on offer and wait for someone to match your request.

There is a huge amount of competition for customers, which means that tax-free betting, low commission rates, initial free bets and bonuses are all offered.

A betting exchange also offers more betting opportunities, such as betting on a photo finish.

The bets can be placed in the privacy of your own home.

You are not punished for winning. With a traditional bookmaker, you are likely to get barred or have your bets limited if you consistently win. However, with a betting exchange you are not playing against the exchange but against other individuals so the exchange does not lose out if you win. They make their money from commission on your bets so the more you bet, the better it is for the exchange.

There is no limit to the size of your bets. As long as you can find a match, you can bet to the level of stakes that your capital allows.

As prices change, you also have the opportunity to hedge bets and lock in a profit.

Disadvantages of using a betting exchange
Big bets cannot always be placed. Bets are limited to the stakes of the players betting. A traditional bookmaker is able to take most high-stake bets but with a betting exchange you are limited by what the other players want to bet.

You can't bet with cash, you need to deposit money with the exchange or use a bank or credit card.

You need to have a computer and internet connection.

Care also needs to be taken to avoid scams, fraud and identity theft.

Types of bet

You can bet on horses to win, lose, place or not place. It is also possible to bet on the winning distance of a horse. Betting on a horse to win is called backing and betting on a horse to lose is called laying. There are two main markets that you can bet on. The win market and the place market. The win market is for horses to win or lose. The place market is for horses to be placed or unplaced.

A place bet is just one bet for the horse to finish in the first two, three or four places depending on how many runners there are. The number of places will depend on how many horses are running and on the firm's rules. As a general guide the number of places paid is usually as follows:

> *5–7 runners first and second*
> *8–15 runners first, second and third*
> *16+ runners (non handicap) first, second and third*
> *16+ runners (handicap) first, second, third and fourth.*

Insight

A bet on a horse being placed is not the same as each way (which is two bets and includes a bet for the horse to win and for it to place). If you want to make an each-way bet with a betting exchange you will need to make two bets – one on the win market and one on the place market.

DECIMAL ODDS

Like the tote at racecourses, the odds are displayed as decimals, with the stake included in the price, so for example 4/1 is 5, evens is 2 and 13/8 is 2.63. The decimals are shown to two places. The table below shows the traditional odds converted to decimal odds.

Converting traditional odds to decimal odds

To convert a traditional price to decimal odds, you add both sides of the price then divide by the number on the right.

For example to convert 4/1 to a decimal:

> *4 + 1 = 5*
> *5 divided by 1 = 5*

To convert 13/8 to a decimal:

> *13 + 8 = 21*
> *21 divided by 8 = 2.625 which is rounded up to 2.63*

Converting decimal odds to traditional odds

To find the traditional odds to one stake unit, deduct 1 from the decimal odds. This then gives you the number on the left of the price to one.

For example, decimal odds of 4.0 are traditional odds of 3/1. Decimal odds of 7.5 are:

> *7.5 – 1 = 6.5 to 1, traditionally shown as 13/2*

Traditional odds	Decimal odds
100/1	101
66/1	67
50/1	51
40/1	41
33/1	34
25/1	26
20/1	21
18/1	19
16/1	17
15/1	16
14/1	15
13/1	14

Traditional odds	Decimal odds
12/1	13
11/1	12
10/1	11
9/1	10
17/2	9.5
8/1	9
15/2	8.5
7/1	8
13/2	7.5
6/1	7
11/2	6.5
5/1	6
9/2	5.5
4/1	5
7/2	4.5
100/30	4.33
3/1	4
11/4	3.75
5/2	3.5
12/5	3.4
9/4	3.25
85/40	3.13
2/1	3
15/8	2.88
7/4	2.75
13/8	2.63
6/4	2.5
7/5	2.4
11/8	2.38
5/4	2.25
6/5	2.2
11/10	2.1
21/20	2.05
1/1 evens	2
20/21	1.9

(Contd)

Traditional odds	Decimal odds
10/11	1.91
5/6	1.83
4/5	1.8
8/11	1.73
4/6	1.67
8/13	1.62
4/7	1.57
8/15	1.53
1/2	1.5
40/85	1.47
4/9	1.45
2/5	1.4
4/11	1.36
1/3	1.33
3/10	1.3
2/7	1.29
1/4	1.25
2/9	1.22
1/5	1.2

HOW THE ODDS ARE SHOWN

The odds are presented in a different way from bookmakers' odds. As different people offer different odds there will be several prices shown for each horse. The odds are presented in the form of a table and displayed from a backer's point of view. The table shows the value of bets that are currently unmatched for a particular price. There are odds displayed for the horses to win and to lose. The odds section of the table is divided into two halves – one half for back odds and the other half for lay odds. The back odds, for the horse to win, are typically listed on the left of the table and the lay odds, for the horse to lose, are on the right. The odds available are arranged in columns. The best odds are usually shown in a coloured or highlighted column.

An example of a betting screen for a betting exchange is shown in the next table, which is headed with the time and place of the race. The table is divided into two halves. The left side shows the back odds and the right side shows the lay odds. Next to the horses' names are several different prices accompanied by an amount. These prices and amounts are arranged in columns. The best current odds are displayed in the column adjacent to the horse's name and are highlighted. In this case, the closer the column is to the outside of the table, the worse the odds. The amount underneath each price is the current maximum that can be bet at those odds. It represents unmatched bets. The amount is the total of all the bets offered at that price. It can be the stakes from more than one person. For example, the 9.8 £54 could be one bet for £50 and one bet for £4.

The prices in the back section are the prices at which you can back horses to win. The amount underneath is how much can currently be bet at that price. Once that amount has been reached, the figure to the left will take its place.

Back			14:30 Ascot	Lay		
4.1	4.2	4.3	Lucky Chance	4.4	4.5	4.6
£2191	£1692	£1558		£1931	£105	£1249
9.8	10	10.5	Dobbin	11	11.5	13.5
£54	£497	£2		£266	£200	£8
17.5	18	18.5	Fast filly	19.5	21	22
£43	£35	£249		£10	£20	£2
15.5	16.5	17	Slow coach	21	22	23
£155	£121	£8		£2	£66	£6

BACK ODDS

In this example the best price available for Dobbin to win is 10.5, the £2 underneath the 10.5 is the amount of unmatched stakes at that price. This means that someone is willing to offer odds of 10.5 for a stake of £2. The next best odds are 10 and it is possible to bet up to £497 at this price. After this the next best odds are 9.8 with up to £54 being available to bet. From a backer's point of view, the highest number is the best price. It represents the multiple of the stake that will be won by the backer if the horse wins.

To back £2 at odds of 10.5, you would click on the price. You will then be taken to a betting screen (the equivalent of a betting slip). The odds of 10.5 will be displayed and there will be a box for you to enter your stake. You enter £2. Your profit (£19) will be displayed. You will then need to confirm the bet in order to place it. On the screen displaying the odds, the price of 10.5 will then disappear and will be replaced by the next best odds of 10 £497. If you decided to bet a further £2 at odds of 10 after making your bet, 10 £495 would now be displayed in the best odds column.

Suppose you want to stake £10 on Dobbin to win, and want to take the best price on offer, you would then bet £2 at odds of 10.5 and £8 at odds of 10.

LAY ODDS

When you lay a bet, you are acting like a traditional bookmaker. If the backer wins (the horse wins), you pay out his winnings but if the backer loses (the horse loses) you win his stake.

Suppose there is 6.0 and £10 on the lay side. If you decide to lay at these odds, you will win £10 if the horse loses. However, like a bookmaker, if the horse wins, you will lose £50.

If you look at the bet in terms of traditional odds, 6 is odds of 5/1. As you are laying the bet, you are taking the place of the bookmaker, you are making the bet of 1/5. In terms of money you lay £50 and the backer stakes £10. The bet from your point of view is £10/£50. You stand to win £10 but in order to win you must stake £50. If you win (i.e. the horse loses) you will get the backer's stake of £10 and keep your stake of £50. If you lose (i.e. the horse wins), the backer will get your £50 stake and will keep his stake of £10.

In the table, the best price available for Dobbin to lose is 11, the £266 underneath the price is the amount of £266 of unmatched bets at a price of 11. The £266 represents bets that have been placed by backers that are currently unmatched. The next best odds are 11.5 and the maximum amount of money that is unmatched is £200. After this the next best odds are 13.5 with £8 being available to bet. From a layer's point of view, the lowest number is the best price. It represents the multiple of the backer's stake that will be lost by the layer if the horse wins. For example, by laying £266 at odds of 11, a layer will win £266 less commission if the horse loses. In order to win this, he needs to stake £2660. If the horse wins, the layer will lose his £2660 stake, which will be paid to the backers.

How bets are matched

A bet is not actually made until it is matched. If someone backs a horse £100 at 5.00 and someone is willing to lay those odds then the bet is matched. A bet may be matched by one or more people. For example, someone may match £60 worth of the bet and another person £40. Once bets are matched they cannot be cancelled.

The bets are held in a queue and are dealt with in the order in which they arrive at the site's server. The queue works on a first come first served basis, so it pays to place bets early in order to get a match. Any bets that are not matched by the start of the race will be void and the stakes refunded. The better the odds that you offer, the more likely you are to get a match.

Insight

With a betting exchange you are not guaranteed that your bet will be placed. If your bet remains unmatched your stake will be refunded.

Suppose you want to stake £10 on Dobbin at odds of 10.5. On
the betting screen, you would enter odds of 10.5 and your stake of
£10:£2 of your bet would be matched and the remaining £8 would
be unmatched. On the lay side of the odds, 10.5 £8 would appear,
with the current best price of 11 £266 moving one place to the
right. Once your 10.5 £8 stake has been matched it will disappear
from the odds screen.

The odds for Dobbin will now show:

9.8	10	Dobbin	10.5	11	11.5
£54	£497		£8	£266	£200

If someone decides to lay these odds, that is bet £8 at 10, your bet
would be matched and the betting screen would now show:

9.8	10	Dobbin	11	11.5	13.5
£54	£497		£266	£200	£8

On your personal account screen it would show that your £10 bet
at odds of 10.5 has been matched. Now that your bet has been
matched it can no longer be cancelled.

Ordering odds

If the odds that you want are not currently available, you can place
an order for them. Your bet may be fully matched, partially matched
or unmatched. If your order is matched then the bet is made. If your
order is not matched by the time of the off then your bet is void.
There is a limit to the odds than can be ordered. Odds lower than
1.01 are not allowed; odds over 1000 are also not allowed.

If, for example, odds of 4.5 are offered for a horse to win and you want odds of at least 5.0 and want to stake £100, then you place an order for odds of 5.0 and offer a stake of £100. If another person is willing to lay at these odds, that is, bet that the horse will lose, then your bet is matched. Your bet can be matched up to your maximum stake of £100. Your bet will be made if someone is prepared to stake £500 that the horse will lose. That is enough to pay out your winnings. What may happen is that your bet is matched with several people's lay bets. For example, one lay bet of £10, one lay bet of £20 and one lay bet of £50. If by the off these are the only three matches then you will have a bet of £80 at odds of 5.0. The additional £20 will be void. If the horse wins, you will receive £420, where £400 is your winnings and £20 is void. Commission will be calculated on the net winnings of £320. At 5 per cent the commission will be £16. You will therefore receive £404.

If you offer odds to other betters you will need to make your odds competitive in order to get a match. To stop ridiculous odds being offered like 1000/1 when the current odds are 5/1, an order can usually only be placed within a certain increment of the current best price. You will need to consult the exchange rules for the increments. For example, you could bet £2 at odds of 10.5 and place an order for £8 at odds of 10.5. Your £8 bet would only be valid if someone else is willing to match it.

9.8	10	10.5	Dobbin	11	11.5	13.5
£54	£497	£2		£266	£200	£8

If you took this option, the 10.5 odds would disappear from the highlighted column to be replaced by the odds of 10. On the lay side, your odds of 10.5 with £8 underneath would appear in the highlighted column where it will remain until someone matches it, that is decides they want to stake £8 at a price of 10.5 that the horse will lose.

9.8 £54	10 £497	Dobbin	10.5 £8	11 £266	11.5 £200

BEST ODDS

If you place a bet at the odds of 6.0 and odds of 6.5 are available then your bet will be matched at these odds as they are better than 6.0. They will not be matched with odds of 5.5 as these are worse odds.

BACK ALL AND LAY ALL

The betting screen also gives you the opportunity to back all the runners.

This is backing the entire field to win, that is, all horses that are running.

Lay all is laying the entire field, that is all the horses, to lose.

OFFICIAL RESULT

All winning bets are settled according to the official result at the time of the 'weigh-in'. This means that if, for example, a horse is later disqualified due to a positive drug test, the result at the 'weigh-in' still counts.

NON-RUNNERS

If a horse is a non-runner, all unmatched and matched bets on the horse are void.

If the race is a walkover (there is only one runner) all bets are void on that race.

If a horse is withdrawn from a race once a market has been formed then, depending on the price of the withdrawn horse, the prices on the remaining horses may be lowered. You are advised to check the betting exchange's rules.

The amount that the price is reduced by is a percentage and called the reduction factor. It is based on the rule 4 system that bookmakers use. Prior to betting on a race, each horse is given a reduction factor based on the exchange's estimates of each horse's chance of winning. Unmatched bets to lay will be cancelled.

In the win market, reductions are made on the whole odds. With a matched bet at odds of 6.00 and a horse with a reduction factor of 20 per cent, your odds will be reduced by 20 per cent and become odds of 4.80.

In a place market, the reduction factor is made to the win portion of the odds. With a reduction factor of 25 per cent, the win portion of the odds will be reduced 25 per cent odds of 8 would become 6.25. For example, for a price of 8, the win portion is the price minus the stake $8 - 1 = 7$; $7 \times 25\% = 1.75$; $8 - 1.75 = 6.25$.

DEAD HEAT

In the event of a dead heat, the odds are divided by the number of declared winners for the market. Suppose two horses dead heat for first place and you have backed one of the winners at a price of 5. You will be paid out at a price of 2.5.

How to bet

From the site's home page, you need to go to the race that you want to bet on. This will take you to the betting screen with the prices. The odds will be constantly changing as more money is bet on a race. Near the off of a race, the situation can quickly change. With some sites, the screen will automatically change to show the new odds but with some you may need to refresh the screen to see the most up-to-date odds.

BETTING OPTIONS

You have several options available to you:

- ▶ *to back a horse at current available odds*
- ▶ *to lay a horse at current available odds*
- ▶ *to place an order for back odds of your choice*
- ▶ *to place an order for lay odds of your choice*
- ▶ *to back all*
- ▶ *to lay all*
- ▶ *to cancel unmatched bets.*

Back a horse to win at current odds

Suppose you want to bet £100 on a horse to win at odds of 2.0 and these odds are available, you place your bet by clicking on the box containing these odds. You will be taken to a screen that is the equivalent of a betting slip. This screen will show the odds and will prompt you to enter your stake. You will then be taken to another screen to confirm your bet.

You have the option of cancelling your bet as long as it is not matched. If just a portion of your bet has been matched, you also have the option of cancelling the unmatched portion. Once a bet has been fully matched it can no longer be cancelled. If the horse wins you will win £200, less commission. If the horse loses, you will lose £100.

Lay a horse to lose at current odds

Suppose you want to lay £100 on a horse to lose. Lay odds of 2.5 are offered and there is £500 unmatched. In order to place a bet, you click on the box containing these odds. You will be taken to a screen that is the equivalent of a betting slip. This screen will show the odds and will prompt you to enter the stake. You need to enter the backer's stake that you are willing to match. You enter £100. Your liability is £150 and will be displayed on the screen. The liability of £150 is how much you will lose if the horse wins. The stake of £100 will be how much you will win from the backer if the horse loses.

Insight

Calculating liability

To calculate your liability you need to deduct one from the decimal price and multiply the remainder by the backer's stake. In the previous example, the decimal price is 2.5. The backer's stake is £100:

2.5 − 1 = 1.5
1.5 × 100 = 150
liability = £150

Calculating commission

The betting exchange charges commission for its services. Commission is typically paid on net winnings at a rate of around 5 per cent. This compares favourably with a traditional bookmaker, where a charge of around 10 to 20 per cent is made.

Examples

You back £100 at 5 and win. Your returns are £500. Your stake is £100. Net profit is 500 − 100 = £400. Commission = 400 × 5% = £20.

Profit after commission = 400 − 20 = £380.

Returns = 380 + 100 = £480.

You lay £100 at 5 and win. Your returns are £100. Your stake is £400. Your returns are £500. Net profit is 500 − 400 = £100. Commission = 100 × 5% = £5. Profit after commission = 100 − 5 = £95.

Returns = 95 + 400 = £495

Book percentage

The book percentage or over-round tells you how profitable a book is. The book percentage is shown for the back and lay markets. It shows how competitive the prices on offer are. It is calculated by adding the individual percentage chance of each selection based on the price that is being offered. A book that is perfectly balanced will have a percentage of 100 per cent. In this case, both backers and layers would break even. If you are laying all selections in a market (like a traditional bookmaker) you should ensure your book percentage is greater than 100 per cent, then you are guaranteed to make a profit. If the book percentage is lower than 100 per cent you will lose money.

If you place bets with a book percentage greater than 100 per cent, and all your bets are matched, you will make money.

If you are backing a selection, you would ideally look for a market where the book percentage was as low as possible, that is as close as possible to 100 per cent. Occasionally a book percentage will go lower than 100 per cent (overbroke). In theory, you could then back every selection and guarantee a profit.

Spread betting

WHAT IS SPREAD BETTING?

Spread betting started about 25 years ago and was used as a way to speculate on the financial markets. Bets were placed on how much the stock exchange would go up or down on a certain day. This form of gambling has been adapted for betting on horse racing.

Instead of betting on individual horses winning or losing, it is betting on combinations of events like how the favourites will perform at a meeting, what the starting prices of all the winning horses will be and what the winning distances will be. The spread betting company will make a prediction about a particular event. You need to decide if their prediction is too high or too low. The more you're right, the more you win and the more you're wrong, the more you lose. Due to its connection with the financial markets, the terms buying and selling are used. Buying is betting higher and selling is betting lower.

It has a higher level of financial risk than traditional betting. With traditional betting you know beforehand how much you will lose if your bet loses. You simply lose the amount you stake. With spread betting, it is possible to have huge losses. To restrict the amount you can lose, it is possible to place a stop order on a bet.

SPREAD BETTING ON FAVOURITES

A spread betting company will give a favourites index at each meeting. This index is based on a score given to favourites that are placed in a race. The scores given can vary but as a general guide a favourite is awarded 25 points for winning, ten points for coming second, five points for third place and no points for finishing in any other position. If there are joint favourites, then the one with the lowest race card number is considered the favourite.

To place a bet, you need to decide whether to bet higher or lower than the predicted score. If, for example, the predicted score is 70 and you think the likely score is higher, then you bet high (buy). If you think the predicted score will be lower, then you bet low.

The payout is calculated on the basis of how much higher or lower the score is.

If you bet £2 high and the result is 85 then you win 15 times your stake: $(85 - 70) \times$ your stake $= 10 \times £2 = £30$.

If you bet low and the result is 80 then you lose ten times your stake: $(80 - 70) \times$ your stake $= 10 \times £2 = -£20$.

JOCKEY PERFORMANCE INDEX

This is a bet on how a jockey performs in a meeting. A jockey is awarded 25 points for winning a race, ten points for coming second, five points for coming third and no points for any other position. The spread betting firm will quote an index for each jockey at the meeting. You need to decide if the result will be higher or lower than the predicted index.

At a race meeting a jockey is predicted as having a performance of 32 to 34 points. You can bet higher than 34 or lower than 32. Suppose you bet £10 lower. If the jockey's score is 25, you win £70. $(32 - 25) \times 10 = £70$.

If the jockey's score is 80, you will lose £460: $(80 - 34) \times 10 = £460$.

STARTING PRICES OF WINNERS

This is a bet on the total of the starting prices (SPs) of all the winners at a race meeting. A 4/1 winner is four points, 10/1 is ten points up to a maximum of 50/1 or 50 points so a 100/1 winner will have 50 points.

The SP prediction may be 55 to 58. If you predict that the result will be higher, you bet high, if you think it will be lower then you bet low.

MATCH BETS

This is a bet on the distance between two nominated horses in a race. The maximum makeup for flat races is 12 lengths and 15 lengths for national hunt. A short head is 0.1 of a length, a head is 0.2 and a neck 0.3, half a length 0.5, ¾ of a length 0.75.

RACE INDEX

This is a bet on an individual horse. Bets are placed on whether or not a horse's index will be higher or lower than the prediction.

The number of points awarded will depend on how many runners there are in a race.

> *For races with over 12 runners:*
> *50 points for first*
> *30 points for second*
> *20 points for third*
> *10 points for fourth*
> *0 points for any other position.*

> *Races with up to 12 runners:*
> *50 points for first*
> *25 points for second*
> *10 points for third.*

> *For example: a horse is predicted to get 13–16 points.*
> *You bet £1 higher at 16. Maximum win is £34, maximum risk is £16.*

> *The horse finishes sixth so has no points. The difference between the price and the result is 16 – 0 = 16. Loss = £1 × 16 = £16.*

DOUBLE RACE CARD NUMBERS

This is a bet based on the total of the winners' doubled race card number at a meeting. For example, if the race card numbers of the winners of a meeting were 2, 5, 11, 7, 3 and 6, this totals 34. The result would be 2 × 34 = 68.

The prediction had been 75–79 and you had bet £10 low (sell). The difference between the result and the prediction is 75 – 68 = 7. Your winnings would be £10 × 7 = £70.

HEAVYWEIGHTS INDEX

Here the performance of the heavyweights is predicted.

Here the total winning margins for a meeting is predicted.

Playing safe

Although internet betting offers greater convenience to the customer it does need to be treated with caution. The internet is a highly competitive business environment and many businesses have been trading for a relatively short time. A number of sites have gone bust owing customers money. Betting on the internet is a relatively new phenomenon and there is a lack of control and legal framework to deal with some problems that may arise. There are also a number of scam sites that have failed to pay out to customers. Be extremely cautious of betting with unregulated sites in foreign jurisdictions. If a site goes bust, it will be virtually impossible for you to get your money back.

You should thoroughly check out an internet betting firm before depositing any money with them. Check that a site is authorized to operate in the country where you are living. Look for a site with a good reputation. There are lots of gambling forums on the internet where gamblers discuss their experiences about internet betting. There are also many sites that give blacklists of companies that have failed to pay out or to treat customers fairly.

Ideally, you should look for a site that is government regulated. Some governments have introduced strict controls for sites operating in their countries. You need to ensure that your money is protected and that the sites are fair. UK firms are strictly regulated and licensed. The major UK high street bookmakers have internet sites and as these companies have built up a good reputation over the years, they are more likely to play fair.

UK betting exchange operators are expected to abide by the code of practice for betting exchanges. This provides a framework for a safe and fair betting environment.

It includes the following provisions:

▶ *That the funds of betting exchange customers should be ring fenced from the operator's funds so that they are segregated at all times.*
▶ *There must always be a reserve fund to clear all accounts at any time.*
▶ *They must adhere to the betting dispute resolution decisions of an external arbitrator, e.g. IBAS (Independent Betting Arbitration Service).*

There are safeguards to allow you to control the amount that you bet. This includes daily/weekly deposit limits that you can decide in advance. They also have self-exclusion schemes that allow you to opt out on request, allowing you to have your account closed for six months.

Look for a site that gives 24/7 support. This ensures that if you have any problems you can contact a member of staff no matter what time of day it is.

Keep your password secret. Anyone who has access to your password could place bets and withdraw money from your bank account or credit card. If you use a computer that is accessible by more than one person, don't save the password so that it can be automatically entered by the computer. Another person using the computer would be able to access your account.

Ensure you use a site where personal information is encrypted. As you may be giving personal details, bank account information and credit card numbers to a site, you will want to be sure that this information is securely transmitted and safely held so that it cannot be accessed by a third party.

PHISHING

Phishing is a method used to obtain a player's password to their internet betting account. What will generally happen is that the victim will get an email, claiming to be from customer support from the betting site. They will give some spurious reason why the customer needs to contact them. The victim will be directed to a web page where it will be necessary to type in his user name and password. The cheater then has the information needed to log in to the victim's account, bet with the money in the account and withdraw winnings.

Government agencies and internet sites are actively working to combat this fraud. The internet site will often quickly be aware that a fraud of this type is being attempted and will send a warning to members or post a warning on the site. If you get an email claiming to be from the betting site, do not click on any of the links posted in the email. Instead, go directly to the site and log on from the site's home page. If you suspect that you have received a phishing email report it directly to the site.

Telephone betting

Telephone betting is placing horse racing bets over the telephone. You will need to open an account with a telephone betting operator. These services are offered by the major UK bookmakers. You will be given a telephone number that will connect you with a call centre. You will be asked a security question to confirm your identity. You can then place your bets verbally. The operator will repeat your bet to confirm the details. Calls are recorded to avoid disputes.

10 THINGS TO REMEMBER

1 *Only bet with reputable online betting firms.*

2 *Take care that you are not a victim of online fraud.*

3 *The odds are displayed as decimals.*

4 *To convert a traditional price to decimal odds, add both sides of the price then divide by the number on the right.*

5 *To convert decimal odds to a traditional price deduct 1 from the decimal odds. This then gives you the number on the left of the price to one.*

6 *The back odds are for the horse to win.*

7 *The lay odds are for the horse to lose.*

8 *Commission of around 5 per cent is deducted from the net winnings.*

9 *The book percentage or over-round tells you how profitable a book is.*

10 *Spread betting is betting on a combination of events like how the favourites will perform at a meeting.*

5

Making your selection

In this chapter you will learn:
* *how to assess the runners*
* *where to find information about the runners*
* *about betting systems.*

Deciding which horse to bet on in a race is not easy. Many factors influence the outcome of horse races. These include things like the jockey, the weight carried, the condition of the ground and the distance of the race. This makes betting on horse racing both interesting and challenging. A gambler needs to use his skill to assess the likely winner and/or placed horses from a field of between two and up to 40 runners.

Even after taking into account all the different factors, some aspects of horse racing are unpredictable. No matter how carefully you have assessed a horse's chances of winning, something can go wrong that can affect the outcome of a race. In national hunt races, horses can be brought down by others. Horses may slip on wet ground. The weights carried by the horse may be lost in the course of the race, causing the horse to be disqualified. Even the jockey's actions may result in a horse being disqualified. Races are run at a fast pace with the jockey making split-second decisions. His actions can result in other horses being impeded, which may lead to disqualification. In his eagerness to make a horse win, he may use his whip more frequently than is allowed under the rules.

A great deal of the information that you need to consider when assessing a horse's chance of winning is given by the race cards printed in newspapers and programmes. The format varies depending on the publication. To save space a lot of abbreviations are used. Take time to familiarize yourself with what all the abbreviations mean.

The analysis of all this information is very time consuming. In recent years several computer programs have been developed to process this information. Using a computer can cut down on the work. There are many different programs on the market, all offering different features, so it is worth shopping around for the best deal.

There is now a wealth of information available over the internet. The amount of information is almost overwhelming. Many online racing magazines, horse racing websites and tipsters services also now exist. Many provide up-to-date analysis of all the statistics, such as performance of favourites, influence of the draw, top trainers, top jockeys and pedigree information.

Factors you can assess

PEDIGREE

For all racehorses, it is possible to trace back their pedigrees for hundreds of years. A good pedigree is an indication of a potentially good horse but not always. Horses are carefully bred to bring out characteristics that make good runners. Horses with good racing records are sent to stud in order to try to bring out those characteristics in future generations. However, due to the nature of genetics, the breeding of these characteristics is not always an exact science. A dam and sire with good racing records do not always produce fast offspring. Often the characteristics that make a good runner can skip generations.

One characteristic that has been shown to have a positive effect on the performance of horses is a large heart. Although this characteristic may be present in the sire, it may not show up in his immediate offspring, only to reappear in later generations. This can mean that a horse that may have had a poor racing record can sire fast offspring. This makes the study of pedigree an inexact method of finding winners. It tends to be used as a tool for finding winners where the horses have not run before.

RUNNERS' PREVIOUS PERFORMANCE

Due to the unpredictability of breeding, a great deal of importance is placed on the previous performance of a horse. Once the horse has actually run, you have a clearer indication of its potential. You will have information available about how the horse has performed in previous races. This is called its form. Different racing publications publish this information in different formats. To cut down on space, abbreviations are used and each publication will give a key explaining them. As a general rule, the more detailed the information, the more you have to pay for it. You will therefore need to decide for yourself how important you feel the information is. The sorts of detail that are given are the results of previous races, the jockey, trainer, weight carried and a guide to the betting. When the horse has not run in many races in the current season, its performance for the previous season will be given.

Try to watch as many races as possible. The written data do not always show why a horse performed poorly. The jockey may have been at fault. He may have waited too long before pushing a horse. A horse may sprint quickly at the end of the race but if the jockey left it too late to push or was boxed in by other horses, it may still lose. A better jockey next time out may compensate.

Some horses may have an easy win, with the jockeys not having to use the whip or, alternatively, easing down near the finish. Other horses may win but under pressure from the jockey. A poorer jockey next time out may mean it loses. A horse could fall at a difficult fence. If the fences are easier in its next race, the horse may not be so unfortunate. A horse may lose a race over the jumps because it is brought down by a loose horse or slips on wet ground.

With better running conditions, it may win its next race. With sprinting races a horse may get off to a bad start. The next race may be better.

At the beginning of the season you will not have a lot of information on which to base your selection. As the season progresses, you will have a much better indication of how the horses are performing. Towards the end of the season, you will have much more consistent data on which to base your decisions. For this reason, you should bet cautiously at the beginning of the season and gradually increase stakes as the season progresses and you are more confident of your selections.

HORSES' SPEED

The speed that a horse can run is by far the clearest indication of how likely a horse is to win. No matter how good the jockey, the trainer or the condition of the ground, if a horse is not fast it is unlikely to win. Assessing the speed is not a simple matter. Factors such as the amount of weight carried and the going all affect a horse's speed.

Insight

In handicap races the speed of a horse will be affected by the weight that it is carrying. You will need to decide if the horse can overcome the weight and still win the race.

Timeform offer the most comprehensive records of the horses' speed. They produce a daily newspaper and separate books giving details of flat racing and national hunt statistics. For anyone seriously assessing a horse's chances of winning, this information is invaluable. (See Taking it further on page 181.) You can, of course, accumulate the information yourself if you are prepared to commit the time it takes to gather data.

HARNESS RACING

The United States Trotting Association keeps records of the fastest race a horse wins each year. Abbreviations are used to cut down on space. With harness racing the comparison of the runners is made easier as most races are run over a mile.

Example: p,3,Q1:58.1($100,000)

p – the horse gait: p = pace, no letter = trot

3 – age of the horse, here it was a 3 year old

Q – the type of race: Q = qualifying race, T = time trial, no letter = during a race

1:58.1 – the time taken to run one mile, in this case one minute and 58⅕ seconds

the length of the track: f = ⅝ mile, s = ⅞ mile, h = ½ mile, no letter = 1 mile

($100,000) – the amount of money won by the horse in its career

THE RACE

You don't have to bet on every race. Save your money for the races that offer the best prospects. It takes time to assess all the runners, so concentrate on a few races each day. Certain races can be dismissed as it is too difficult to predict the outcome. It is better to select races where you have a clear indication of a horse's performance. Avoid selling races, claiming races, maiden handicaps, apprentice races and amateur races. With the higher class races you will have a lot more information on which to base your decision. Clips of the horses' previous races run will be shown by the racing media and a lot more information will be written over these horses in horse racing publications.

DISTANCE OF THE RACE

Most horses have an optimum distance over which they perform
well. Some are excellent sprinters while others have stamina to
cope with longer distances. If a horse is entered for a distance that
it has never run before, its previous performance can provide some
indication as to how well it will fare. Has the horse run shorter
distances and won easily? Or has it run longer distances but lacked
stamina and faded at the end? If you watch lots of racing you will
notice these factors.

CHANGE OF CLASS

The grade of race may have an effect on the outcome of a race. If a
horse performs particularly well in, for example, a Class 2 race, it may
be entered for a Class 1 race. Since Class 1 races attract the best horses,
it will be up against much stronger opposition than in its previous race.
Avoid betting on horses that have moved up a class. Wait for them to
prove themselves in their new class. It is also possible for horses to
drop down a grade so a horse that has previously run in a Class 1
race may compete in a Class 2 race. The horse may have performed
badly in the Class 1 race but the change of class may lead to a huge
improvement. The form guides in newspapers give details of which
horses are running in different classes.

RUNNERS' EXPERIENCE

Races in which the horses have never run before are notoriously
difficult to pick the winners. The problem with betting on them is
that you have no previous form on which to base your assessment.
This is where the pedigree of the horse needs to be studied. You
can glean the horse's potential by studying the racing records of
its parents, the dam and sire. A much clearer indication can be
achieved by going back several generations. They may also have
produced other offspring that have already run which gives you
more information on which to base your selection. The trainer,
jockey and owner will also play a role in your selection.

A horse's experience can be particularly important over jumps. An inexperienced horse that has only recently been trained to jump is more likely to fall than one with more experience.

Flat races where the horses must start in stalls can cause problems. Experienced horses are more used to the stalls and less likely to be nervous. A nervous horse can easily injure itself and/or the jockey in the stalls or simply refuse to race once it has been let out. You will also know of experienced horses that are nervous in the stalls.

Although an older horse has more experience, it may also be less fit than its rivals. You will need to decide at what stage the age of a horse becomes a negative factor. This is not always easy as some horses do have exceptional records even at an old age. Red Rum was 12 years old when he won his third Grand National. In 1980 Sonny Somers won two steeplechases at the age of 18. The record for the oldest horse ever to win a race is held by Marksman who won a flat race at Ashford in 1826 at the age of 18.

CONDITION OF THE GROUND ('THE GOING')

The condition of the ground on the racecourse is called the going. Before the start of racing the clerk of the course will inspect the condition of the ground and declare the going. The going is classified from the fastest to the slowest conditions as follows:

- ▶ *hard*
- ▶ *firm*
- ▶ *good to firm*
- ▶ *good*
- ▶ *good to soft*
- ▶ *soft/yielding*
- ▶ *heavy.*

Since courses do not drain evenly there may be patches of ground where the going differs from the rest of the course. For example, you may see the going quoted as 'good (good to firm patches)'.

In order to get more consistent ground, some tracks are watered. On all-weather tracks where the racing surface is made of fibre-sand, the going is fairly consistent and is quoted as standard.

The condition of the ground may affect how well a horse runs. For example, some run well on heavy ground, while others run poorly. You will have to ask yourself if the ground suits your selection. A horse may have won its last race on hard ground but if its next race is on heavy ground, you will need to assess what impact this change will have. By going back through the records you can see how well a horse performed on particular ground. If you attend a race meeting, you will be able to inspect the ground yourself and draw your own conclusions about how it will affect the horses.

Insight

A good time for betting can be towards the end of the flat season when the ground has usually dried out. This removes one of the unknown factors. Also by this stage the performance of the horses is known. This is traditionally a time of year when the bookmakers start losing money.

WEATHER CONDITIONS

Always take note of the weather forecast. If it is expected to rain, bear in mind that the going may change. Ground that started out as good, can easily become heavy after a huge downpour. Some horses fare better than others depending on the weather conditions. Hot weather has a more adverse effect on bigger horses than it does on small ones.

THE COURSE

In the United States, racetracks are of less importance, as they are mostly the same oval-shaped dirt tracks. In Great Britain where all courses are different, this can also have an effect on how well a horse runs. Some courses have left-hand bends and others right. Some are flat. Others have slight inclines and some steep hills.

You will need to consider how the racecourse is going to affect a horse. The horse you select may have a preference for right-hand turns; therefore you will need to assess the impact of a course with left-hand turns. A horse may run well on a flat course, but how is a hill going to affect his performance?

Starting stalls are used in flat racing to ensure that each horse starts at precisely the same time. The draw is the position in which the horse starts in the stalls – not to be confused with its race card number. At a lot of racecourses there are advantages to starting in certain positions in the stalls.

BLINKERS

Some horses are distracted by other horses and so do not run well. Blinkers are an aid that allow a horse to only see in front of it, with the other runners excluded from its vision. If a horse is wearing blinkers for the first time, it is possible for there to be a marked improvement in its running.

CONDITION OF THE HORSE

In the course of racing and training horses may get injured. Nowadays veterinary care is of the highest quality with excellent treatment available. The effect of an injury on a horse's future performance can be negligible. However, some horses may have recurrent injury problems that can make their performance unreliable. Keeping up to date with all the news will highlight any horses that are not entirely fit. Be wary of horses that are running after a long absence as they may have been injured or ill. They may have previously had good form but the impact of an injury or illness will need to be assessed.

Pregnancy (in foal) can be a big advantage to a horse. This is due to an increase in red blood cells that allows more oxygen to be carried to the muscles, which increases their efficiency, meaning a horse can run much faster.

THE OWNER

The owner of a horse can also be included in your assessment. Some owners have a particularly good reputation for spotting and buying good-quality horses with the potential to win races. Your knowledge about owners can also help with the selection of horses on their first outing. If a particular owner has a good record of winners, a horse on its first outing entered in a race by him may have a better chance of winning than novices of other owners.

THE TRAINER

All trainers are different. They employ a variety of methods for training horses – some are better than others. Some trainers also have a good reputation for bringing out the very best in a horse. You will need to keep up to date with the latest news to discover which trainers are producing winners. Another important factor is a change of trainer. A new trainer may improve the performance of a horse.

THE JOCKEY

Avoid unproven jockeys. Over shorter distances the jockey is less crucial. With longer distances, experienced jockeys will generally fare better as tactics play a part in the outcome. They will be better at pacing a race and keeping out of trouble. Stick to experienced jockeys over the jumps. An inexperienced jockey is more likely to fall off or pull up.

Keep up to date with jockey changes. A jockey may become ill or injured resulting in a horse having a different rider. The replacement may be better or worse so you will need to review your selection.

NUMBER OF RUNNERS

If you are making place or each-way bets keep up to date with the number of runners. A bet may not be worthwhile if you only get 1/5 odds instead of 1/4. A rule 4 deduction can also impact on your bet.

Factors you cannot assess

Because horse racing is unpredictable, things can and do go wrong. All the studying in the world cannot guard against this.

HORSES CAN HAVE OFF-DAYS TOO

Horses can be unpredictable. Even the most well-behaved horses can have off-days. If they don't want to co-operate with a jockey they will:

▶ *dig their heels in and refuse to run*
▶ *not go into the starting stall*
▶ *refuse to jump fences*
▶ *attempt to throw a jockey off.*

You may know in advance that a horse has a reputation for being difficult, so it's best to avoid betting on it. Save your money for the runners you are certain of.

OTHER HORSES

It is common for horses to bring down others at jumps. A horse may be the best jumper in the world but if another horse gets in its way, it can easily fall. Loose horses can cause all sorts of problems. They can box in your selection, bump into it or run across its path, all of which can cause a horse to lose a race.

WEIGHTS

Weights can and do occasionally fall off in the course of a race. Jockeys also sometimes forget to weigh in after a race. Either of these situations results in disqualification.

FALSE STARTS

A false start can ruin a horse's chance of winning – he may have run half of the race before being recalled. However, safeguards have been put in place to prevent a repeat performance of the 1993

British Grand National fiasco when several horses completed the course after a false start.

OTHER FACTORS

Jockeys do occasionally take the wrong course. Horses can also escape from the jockey before the race. This can result in their being withdrawn from the race, particularly if they have used up a lot of energy running all over the course. Although you will have your stake refunded (unless you've bet ante-post (see page 45)), if that horse is your selection, it can mean your hard work has been wasted. Alternatively, if your horse is still running, it can mean that adjustments to the betting make your bet unprofitable (if, for example, you have bet each way).

Insight

Although these incidents do not happen frequently, you should bear them in mind as possibilities. It's tempting to stake a lot of money on a horse when you think it can't fail to win. By keeping your stakes to a reasonable level on each race, you will minimize your losses when these events do occur.

Gathering information

A lot of information is given by the race cards printed in newspapers or programmes. The format varies depending on the publication. To save space lots of abbreviations are used.

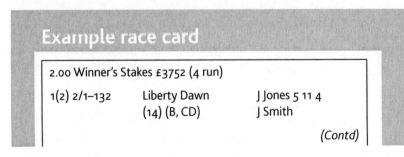

Example race card

2.00 Winner's Stakes £3752 (4 run)

1(2) 2/1–132	Liberty Dawn (14) (B, CD)	J Jones 5 11 4 J Smith

(Contd)

2(3)	Bronze Cannon	F Evans 4 10 10
		D Bolton
3(1)	111 Lucky Luc (28)	S Moon 4 10 10
		S Heard
4(4)	Suzie's Boy	G Chip 5 11 4
		K Bearman

Betting: 2 Lucky Luc, 4 Liberty Dawn, 10 Bronze Cannon, Suzie's Boy

---

2.00	– time of the race
Winner's Stakes	– name of the race
£3752	– prize money to the winning owner
(4 run)	– number of runners
1	– race card number
(2)	– draw – position in starting stalls
01–132	– the horse's form in its last six races

1 =1st, 2 = 2nd, 3 = 3rd, 0 = unplaced, d = disqualified

A dash (–) is a break of one season. An oblique (/) indicates two or more seasons' break. The figure on the right is the latest race. In national hunt racing the following abbreviations are also used: U = unseated rider; F = fell; B = brought down; P = pulled up; R = refused.

Liberty Dawn	– the name of the horse
(14)	– number of days since it last ran
(B, CD)	– meanings of abbreviations follow:

B = horse was wearing blinkers, headgear that restricts lateral vision
V = visor, blinkers that minimize awareness of activity on either side
H = hood
E = eyeshield
B* = blinkers worn for the first time
BF = beaten favourite last time out
C = winner over the course
D = winner over the distance

CD	– course and distance winner
J Jones	– name of trainer
Betting	– rough guide to what the betting is likely to be
5 11 4	– a 5-year-old horse, carrying 11 stone 4
J Smith	– name of jockey

LEARN ABOUT HORSE RACING

Become knowledgeable about horse racing. Read as many publications as possible. Ensure that you have a thorough understanding of the subject. Keep up to date with the latest news by reading a good quality racing newspaper (see Taking it further on page 181 for details of racing publications). The more information you have, the better able you are to assess a horse's chance of winning.

Keep your own records on the horses you are interested in. Use a diary to record events as they happen. You may notice something that others have missed.

TIPSTERS

Studying all these factors takes an enormous amount of time. If you lack the time to do it yourself there are other people who have already done all of the hard work. They are the tipsters employed by the newspapers. They select the likely prospects that they think will win. There are also lots of telephone and internet tipping services that charge for information.

However, you don't always know what system they're using to assess the horses and how good that system is. They may have missed an important factor that you may have noticed. The newspapers boast when their tipsters get it right but keep quiet when they don't – after all, they are in the business of selling newspapers. Over the course of the year tipsters get it wrong too.

RECORD PREDICTORS

The record for predicting the most winners in one day is held
by Charles Lamb, racing correspondent for the *Baltimore News
American*. In 1974, he picked out ten winners at a meeting held at
Delaware Park. Bob Butcher of the *Daily Mirror* correctly forecast
seven winners for a meeting at Wolverhampton. So, too, did
Fred Shawcross at a York meeting in 1988.

Systems

Looking through the small ads of publications will often turn up
a number of advertisements for betting systems. There are lots of
different systems. They often guarantee excellent returns.

Do they work? The sellers of systems will tell you they do. Friends
will boast that they have invented the ultimate system that never
fails. Throughout the years many systems have been invented, some
more successful than others.

Ignore all claims that are made about a system. To test how
effective it is, try it out yourself on a dummy run. Don't bet any
money. Make a note of results over a period of time and apply the
system to those results. If it gives good returns, then try it with
small stakes. Continue to monitor results. If it starts failing, then
give up on it and try something else.

DEVELOPING YOUR OWN SYSTEMS FOR SELECTING HORSES

Try to develop your own systems for selecting horses to bet on.
You will need to take account of all the influencing factors
mentioned. Some are more important than others but all play
a part. One method is to award points for each factor. Most
importance should be placed on the speed of a horse, with points
added for factors that have a positive influence and points
deducted for those that have a negative influence.

DOUBLING UP ON THE FAVOURITE

Some systems involve no assessment of the runners. A popular system is doubling up on the favourite. Here, a bet is placed on the favourite in the first race. If that loses, the stake is doubled and placed on the favourite in the second race. This continues until there is a winner and the gambler stops betting.

This system falls down in several ways. The capital required to make it work can be huge. It may be some time before a favourite wins (they lose around 60 per cent of their races). If the favourite is a very low price (below 6/5), you will not recoup your outlay. There is always the danger that a horse could be withdrawn. This could bring the price of the favourite below the level that you need to break even. The potential rewards are also low.

Example

▶ *First race £10 bet stake = £10.90. Total loss £10.90.*
▶ *Second race £20 bet stake = £21.80. Total loss £32.70.*
▶ *Third race £40 bet stake = £43.60. Total loss £76.30.*
▶ *Fourth race £80 bet stake = £87.20. Total loss £163.50.*

In the fourth race the favourite wins at 1/2. Returns = £120.
Total loss = £43.50.
If the favourite had won at 2/1, returns = £240.
Total winnings = £76.50.

However, there is no guarantee that the favourite would win by the fourth race. If your stake becomes too high, a bookmaker may refuse your bet. You may also run out of capital before a favourite wins.

During the last few minutes before a race, prices can change drastically. Instead of there being just one favourite, a situation can arise where there are joint or even co-favourites. Where you just back the favourite without specifying the name of the horse, your winnings will be greatly reduced if the race is won by a joint or co-favourite. In a situation where there are co-favourites of four, your winnings would only amount to a quarter of what you had expected. Since favourites' prices are low, you are unlikely to recoup your outlay.

Some people apply the system to second favourites because their prices are higher. The problem here is that second favourites win fewer races than favourites, so the capital needed is greater.

Insight

With this system, you are also making no assessment of the runners. By properly considering the chances of each horse, you may discover that another horse is more likely to win the race.

BETTING ON HORSES THAT HAVE TRAVELLED A LONG DISTANCE TO RACE

The logic of this is that a trainer wouldn't travel several hundred miles if the horse didn't stand a good chance of winning. The problem with this system is that there may be an equally good horse in the race that has only travelled a short distance. Horses do travel all over the world. British horses are taken to America and France. However, this doesn't mean that they are guaranteed to win.

BETTING ON HORSES THAT HAVE AN ADVANTAGE ON THE DRAW

With a lot of British racecourses, the draw can have an effect on the race. Horses starting in certain positions in the stalls have an advantage over others. By combining your assessment of horses with this knowledge, it is possible to select several horses that have a good chance of winning. Instead of backing the horses to win, bets of combination tricasts are placed.

A tricast is predicting which horses will finish first, second and third in the correct order. For a small outlay, the returns are potentially huge.

A particularly good time of the year to play this bet is in the summer months when the ground has dried out and the form is starting to show through. At this time of year it is much easier to assess the horses. You do not have to worry about the going and you have lots of previous races on which to make your judgement.

Insight

In the 1980s bookmakers started to lose a lot of money through this system. Many were also offering huge bonuses of around 20 per cent on correct tricasts, which increased their losses. They are now extremely cautious about accepting bets on combination tricasts, particularly where the stakes are large. In order to get your bet accepted, you may need to spread it around several bookmakers.

Effect of the draw at British and Irish racecourses

- ▶ Ascot: *no significant advantage.*
- ▶ Ayr: *6 furlongs in large field – middle numbers; 7 furlongs and over – low numbers.*
- ▶ Bath: *sprints – low numbers.*
- ▶ Beverley: *5 furlong course – high numbers.*
- ▶ Brighton: *sprints – low numbers.*
- ▶ Carlisle: *high numbers; however low numbers are favoured when the going is soft.*
- ▶ Catterick: *low numbers.*
- ▶ Chepstow: *straight course – high numbers; round course – low numbers.*
- ▶ Chester: *round course 7½ furlongs – low numbers.*
- ▶ Curragh: *high numbers.*
- ▶ Doncaster: *round course – no advantage; straight course – low numbers.*

- ▶ Dundalk: *no advantage.*
- ▶ Edinburgh: *7 furlongs and 1 mile races – high numbers.*
- ▶ Epsom: *up to 8½ furlongs – low numbers.*
- ▶ Fairyhouse: *no advantage.*
- ▶ Folkestone: *straight 6 furlong course – low numbers.*
- ▶ Galway: *high numbers.*
- ▶ Goodwood: *sprint races – high numbers.*
- ▶ Gowran Park: *no advantage.*
- ▶ Hamilton Park: *straight course – middle to high numbers.*
- ▶ Haydock Park: *6 furlongs to 1 mile – low numbers; if going soft on straight course – high numbers.*
- ▶ Kempton Park: *round course – high numbers.*
- ▶ Killarney: *no advantage.*
- ▶ Laytown: *no advantage.*
- ▶ Leicester: *straight course up to 1 mile – middle to high numbers (even more so on soft ground).*
- ▶ Leopardstown: *slight advantage to low number.*
- ▶ Lingfield Park: *straight course – high numbers if the going is heavy, otherwise low numbers.*
- ▶ Newbury: *no advantage.*
- ▶ Newcastle: *no advantage.*
- ▶ Newmarket: *no advantage.*
- ▶ Nottingham: *straight course – high numbers; round course – low numbers.*
- ▶ Pontefract: *sprints – low numbers.*
- ▶ Redcar: *sprints – high numbers.*
- ▶ Ripon: *straight course – low numbers; round course – high numbers.*
- ▶ Salisbury: *if the going is soft – low numbers.*
- ▶ Sandown Park: *5 furlong course – high numbers when the going is soft.*
- ▶ Thirsk: *straight course – high numbers; round course – low numbers.*
- ▶ Warwick: *races up to 8 furlongs – high numbers (more marked when the going is soft).*
- ▶ Windsor: *sprints – high numbers; on soft ground – low numbers.*
- ▶ Wolverhampton: *no advantage.*

- ► Yarmouth: *straight course – high numbers; round course – low numbers.*
- ► York: *soft ground – low numbers; over 7 furlongs – low numbers.*

PRICE

Look for horses that offer good value prices. Finding 10/1 winners will give you bigger profits than odds-on, low-priced horses.

SUMMARY

- ► *Concentrate your efforts on a few races each day.*
- ► *Assess recent form of a horse.*
- ► *Place emphasis on the speed of a horse.*
- ► *Avoid betting on horses that have moved up a class.*
- ► *Avoid unproven jockeys.*
- ► *Look for horses that have run recently.*
- ► *Take account of the draw.*
- ► *Bear in mind the quality of a horse's previous opponents: an easy win last time out may just be the result of poor opposition.*
- ► *Be cautious at the beginning of the season and make small bets. Once the form is established increase stakes. Make bigger bets towards the end of a season when the form is more reliable.*
- ► *Avoid low-grade races, courses and horses. There will be more information on the best horses that will help you to make a better decision.*
- ► *Look for horses that offer value bets.*

10 THINGS TO REMEMBER

1 *The pedigree is useful for assessing horses that have not run before.*

2 *The form is a record of how horses have performed in previous races.*

3 *The speed of a horse is one of the clearest indications of how likely a horse is to win.*

4 *The going is the condition of the ground.*

5 *The going may change depending on the weather conditions.*

6 *Keep up to date with jockey changes.*

7 *Consider if the distance of the race is optimum for your selection.*

8 *The draw can influence the outcome of the race.*

9 *Be aware of the factors you cannot assess.*

10 *If betting each-way, keep up to date with the number of runners. This will affect the odds paid.*

6

Betting tips

In this chapter you will learn:
- *how bookmakers make a profit*
- *about setting a budget*
- *how to make the best bet*
- *about getting the best odds*
- *about hedging*
- *about dutching.*

Winning at horse racing involves a lot more than simply selecting the best horses. Lots of factors have an influence on how profitable you will be. We have already seen how bookmakers make a profit. Around 17 per cent of betting turnover is guaranteed to go to them regardless of the race result. If you bet with an exchange or spread betting firm you will need to overcome the commission, which is between 1 and 5 per cent. In order to win at horse racing you need to find a way of betting that overcomes these factors and gives you a profit on your stakes.

Be aware of rules

When you place a bet make sure you fully understand the rules. Each year, a small fortune in winning bets is not claimed. This is often due to betters misunderstanding the rules. Bets where the punter must write out a betting slip as in Great Britain are particularly prone to mistakes. A bet may illegible, incorrectly written or wrongly timed. Ask for a copy of the rules and take them home and study them.

As well as the betting rules, learn the rules that apply to horse racing. If you bet at a racecourse and there is a stewards' enquiry, there could be an amended result. While the enquiry is in progress, the bookmakers will often lay odds on the outcome. If you saw the incident that led to the enquiry and have a thorough knowledge of horse racing, you can use this to your advantage and bet on the outcome.

Appreciate your chances of winning

Have a thorough understanding of the odds against winning. The prices offered by bookmakers are not the realistic chances a horse has of winning. The bookmaker has adjusted the odds to allow himself to make a profit. If you learn how to calculate the profit on a book, you can judge whether or not it is worth having a bet.

How bookmakers make a profit

The prices change constantly as more bets are placed. A big bet on a horse will result in its price being lowered. If horses are not attracting bets, prices will be increased.

Bookmakers aim to make a profit on each race. On average the minimum profit on each race is around 17 per cent. For some books, the profit may be slightly less and for others it will be much greater. To find out if you are getting value for money, you can calculate how much profit the bookmaker is taking. You may decide that it is not worthwhile betting because the bookmaker's profit is too high.

CALCULATING THE PROFIT

1 *Apply the following formula to each price:*

$$\frac{100 \times b}{(a + b)}$$

   a = the number on the left of the price

   b = the number on the right of the price.

2 *Add together the amounts found in 1.*
3 *Deduct 100.*

The balance is the percentage profit made by the bookmaker.

Example

A three-horse race may initially have the following prices:

A 1/2
B 2/1
C 5/1

1 **A** $\dfrac{100 \times 2}{(1 + 2)} = 66.66$

   B $\dfrac{100 \times 1}{(2 + 1)} = 33.33$

   C $\dfrac{100 \times 1}{(5 + 1)} = 16.66$

2 66.66 + 33.33 + 16.66 = 116.65
3 116.65 − 100 = 16.65

Here the bookmaker is making 16.65 per cent profit. This is around the 17 per cent mark. Where the profit is greater than 17 per cent, you are not getting good value for money. The lower the bookmaker's profit, the better it is for you.

Insight

Races with fewer runners give smaller profits for bookmakers and are consequently better for gamblers. This is because there are fewer runners on which the bookmaker can add his profit. And, conversely, races with a large number of runners give bigger profits.

One of the reasons why it is so important to assess the prices of the horses yourself is that sometimes the bookmakers can get the odds wrong. If you can spot this, you are more likely to win.

Two former betting shop managers realized that the odds offered by bookmakers for getting a hole in one in golfing championships was much higher than the actual chances. The true odds of a hole in one in major tournaments were around 2/1. Some bookmakers had not properly assessed the chances and were offering odds as high as 100/1. This represented a huge difference and was worth betting on. The two men gave up work and travelled around the UK betting with small bookmakers on this event. Over the course of a year they staked £30,000 and won approximately £500,000. Once the bookmakers realized their error it was too late, although some did refuse to pay out.

It is unlikely to happen again with holes in one on golf as everyone is aware of the true situation now, but a situation could arise where the bookmaker has failed to make a proper assessment of all the odds. By using the formulae for assessing probability and calculating odds, you can check if a bookmaker is getting it right.

Keep records of your gambling

Try to keep accurate records of your betting. Also, write down the reasons why you win or lose. Analyse your results periodically.

By keeping records, you will be in a much better position to assess your betting strategy and to make changes if it is not effective.

ILLEGAL GAMBLING

If you bet legally you can ensure that you are fairly treated. However, by betting illegally you have no guarantee. There are several problems with illegal bookmakers. They may simply take your money and run or refuse to pay you. Since gambling debts are not recoverable through the courts, there is nothing you can do about it.

Alternatively, the illegal bookmaker may offer you credit. If your bets lose, your credit is increased. Gradually your debts accumulate. Then the bookmaker turns nasty. He wants his money back and he starts charging an extortionate amount of interest on the balance that your owe. He cannot get his money through legal action, so he may go to any lengths to get you to pay up.

Set a budget

Calculate your disposable income by deducting your living expenses from your income. Then decide how much of your disposable income you can comfortably afford to lose. The amount you have calculated is your budget for gambling.

Be sure to stick to your budget. Never be tempted to make additional bets from, for example, your rent money. If you keep to your budget you can gamble with the knowledge that no matter how much you lose, you will not go bankrupt.

Even if your budget is small, you can still enjoy betting on horse racing. The minimum stakes are low. In a betting shop, you can place a bet for as little as 20p. People betting low stakes make up the majority of a betting shop's customers. Another way to make your money go further is from a betting syndicate with other gamblers.

This enables you to pool your knowledge with the other members of the syndicate and to place a greater range of bets than you could normally afford.

When you go out gambling take only your stake money and enough for your expenses (fare home, drinks, meals, etc.). Leave all chequebooks and cash cards at home. If you can't get your hands on more money, you can't spend it. Don't be tempted to borrow money from friends. Decline all offers of credit. If you run out of money, either go home or just watch the racing.

If you don't want to carry large amounts of cash, open a separate bank account for your gambling money and take with you only the chequebook and cards relating to that account when you gamble. By having a sensible approach to gambling you can ensure that you don't lose more than you can afford.

Also take extra care if you have a big win. It is not necessary to take all your winnings in cash. Accepting a cheque from the bookmaker for all or part of the winnings is much safer than carrying around large amounts of cash, which can easily be stolen from you.

When you have a big win do not be tempted to start placing large bets. It's very tempting as soon as you collect your winnings to place a large bet on the next race. If you haven't properly assessed the race, you are simply relying on luck alone. It is best to stick to your tried and tested methods and to bet only when you are certain that you have a good chance of winning.

Staying in control

There are many issues that you need to consider before you bet. You may already know some gamblers; they have probably recounted stories of their big wins. However, it is highly unlikely that they have told you how much money they have lost. A lot of gamblers will tell you that they always break even; if this is true, why do bookmakers make such huge profits? No matter what other gamblers tell you, do not assume that it is easy to win.

Gambling is risky. You can easily lose. No matter how well you have assessed the runners, there are always unpredictable things that can happen. Your horse may be brought down by a loose horse or the jockey could inadvertently take the wrong course, which would lead to disqualification. When gamblers start losing there is a tendency to try to recoup losses by betting more heavily. Most people are able to keep the level of their gambling under control without it becoming a problem. However, for some people, it can become addictive, leading to financial ruin and family breakdown. If you find that your betting is getting out of control, you should contact one of the gambler's help organizations. Details are given on page 181.

You can recognize that you have a problem if you:

- ▶ *view betting as a way of earning money*
- ▶ *continually exceed your budget*
- ▶ *bet money that was intended for living costs*
- ▶ *borrow money for betting*
- ▶ *take days off work to bet*
- ▶ *spend all your free time betting*
- ▶ *find your betting interferes with family life.*

Gambler's help organizations are able to offer solutions. Many have a telephone helpline where you speak to a councillor. They also hold meetings where gamblers can discuss their problems and find solutions. There are also organizations that support the families of gamblers. Your general practitioner will also be able to offer advice on counselling.

Some betting firms also offer self-exclusion schemes. During the period of self-exclusion they will not take bets from you.

Take account of all costs

As well as the cost of your bets, there will be additional expenses that you need to include.

BETTING TAX AND OTHER DEDUCTIONS

In many countries, there is some sort of taxation applied to horse racing. The horse racing industry, racetracks and horse racing associations also often take a cut of betting turnover. The deductions applied to horse racing vary around the world between zero and as much as 24 per cent. Tote betting commonly has the biggest deductions. In the United States, deductions vary from 15–25 per cent for single bets and 19–35 per cent for multiple bets. Irish betting shops charge a 5 per cent tax. Offshore betting operators offer tax-free betting, however they make a service charge, which is typically 3–5 per cent. There is tax-free betting with bookmakers at British and Irish racecourses.

If you bet with an on-course bookmaker and are betting each way, pay particular attention to how many places and what fraction of the odds they are offering as some offer better deals than others. The bookmakers also offer additional bets, like betting on the outcome of a photo finish or stewards' enquiry, so it is worth getting a good view of the race. If you see an incident happen at close quarters you can make yourself some extra money by betting on it.

The bookmakers on the course are independent so you will find that they will all be offering slightly different prices. Each bookmaker has his own book to balance, so the prices he offers will depend on what bets he has personally taken. It's worthwhile taking your time to shop around for the best price for your selection. However, do not take too long to decide where to bet as the prices can change quickly.

ADMISSION CHARGES

Although British and Irish racecourses offer tax-free betting, this can often be offset by admission fees and travelling costs.

The admission charges vary, increasing when prestigious meetings are held. These costs can be reduced by joining a racing club or by organizing group outings to gain discounts on admission and to reduce travelling costs.

SPORTING NEWSPAPERS

A good-quality racing newspaper is essential to glean all the up-to-date racing news. Details of racing publications can be found at the end of the book in the Taking it further section. Using library and betting shop copies can eliminate this cost. An enormous amount of information also appears on the internet, which is ideal for the latest news.

REFRESHMENTS

If you go to a race meeting, taking a picnic is part of the social occasion and is much cheaper than eating in a restaurant. Avoid drinking alcohol as it impairs your judgement and makes you inclined to bet more recklessly.

PHONE CALLS

Many bookmakers offer facilities for customers to bet over the telephone. You will need to take into account the cost of the calls, which can add up to a considerable expense over a period of time. Try shopping around, as some bookmakers offer free calls, which saves a lot of money.

Telephone results and tipster services are charged at a premium rate, so can be costly. Although they are convenient to use, it is much cheaper to check results and get tips from other sources like newspaper, teletext and the radio.

YOUR TIME

Your time can be one of the costliest parts of gambling. To be profitable you will often have to devote an enormous amount of time to assessing runners. Each horse, jockey and trainer's performance needs to be looked at in detail. A horse's preference for different ground also needs to be taken into consideration. Up-to-date records are essential. Yesterday's results can completely change the picture. Gathering all this information takes time. So, too, does analysing it.

You can cut down on the amount of time needed by forming a syndicate. The task of assessing the runners can then be divided between the members (see page 142).

BANK CHARGES

If you are betting over the internet or telephone, you may incur bank charges for transferring money to or from your betting account.

Be selective

You do not have to bet on every race. It pays to be selective; this way your money will last longer. Carefully choose the races that you bet on. Not every race offers good betting opportunities. Some races are simply too competitive making it extremely hard to select the winner. If a race is too competitive, ignore it. Your assessment of the horses may only find a few bets each week that are worth making. By only betting on horses that have a realistic chance of winning, you will increase your profits. Any new strategy should be tested initially with low stakes. It can be costly if the stakes are high and the strategy is not effective. If you have a losing streak, stop betting and reassess your strategy.

Take your time

Don't wait until the day of the race to assess the runners. You can do this in advance as the race cards are published ahead of time.

Take your time and give careful consideration to your selections. This gives you time to assess the horses competing in forthcoming races.

Maximize returns

It is not just necessary to identify winners. To gain as big as profit as possible you need to identify big price winners. Remember the prices on offer reflect the amount of money bet on them. They are not the chances that a horse has of winning. In the Grand National four horses have won at odds of 100/1. A high-priced winner is clearly more profitable than one at a low price.

Many people assume that if they are backing a high-priced horse, they should reduce their stakes. This is not true. If your selection has a high price, back it at your usual stake level.

Be realistic

- ▶ *Don't expect to win on every race.*
- ▶ *Don't bet your entire stake on one horse.*
- ▶ *A spread of bets is less risky.*
- ▶ *If you start losing, don't be tempted to make big bets to recoup your losses.*

How bookmakers try to make you spend more money

Betting shops are in business to make a profit. They want you to spend as much time as possible on their premises. To keep you there they try to make the shops as comfortable as possible. Refreshments are usually available so that you need not leave if you are hungry or thirsty.

There is always something for you to bet on. Greyhound racing is interspersed with the horse racing to get you to bet as much as possible. It also starts earlier than the horse racing and finishes later to try to encourage you to bet both while you put on your bets before the horse racing starts and when you are collecting any winnings at the end of the horse racing. Sports betting is also heavily advertised. Many sporting events are also televised in the shops to encourage you to stay and bet.

The staff is trained to tempt you to switch to bets that are more profitable for the bookmaker. Each day there are special offer bets advertised with bonuses and consolations. They are always the types of bet that give the bookmakers the biggest profits. Often example bets are shown written on the whiteboards. Again, they are the bets that are highly profitable for the bookmaker. On major race days, vouchers are often given away for free bets that can be used the following week. This is to ensure that you come back.

The betting slips for the most profitable bets are colourful and prominently displayed. Instructions for completing the slip are printed on them. However, if you want to make a bet that is more profitable for you, it has to be written on a blank slip. No instructions are supplied.

Competitions that are usually free to enter are often run. The most common type is for the customer to select one horse each day. The customer who has theoretically won the most money by the end of the week wins a prize. This ensures that you visit the betting shop every day. The bookmaker knows that as soon as you are on the premises you are likely to have a bet.

Everything is designed with profit in mind, even the way the newspapers are displayed. The greyhound cards are arranged nearest the counter where the bets are placed. This ensures that you do not have too far to go when the hare is running (a race is about to start). The main meetings of the day are usually placed opposite the screens. This means you can look at the prices and when you turn around the race card for the meeting is directly opposite you.

The tipsters' boxes on the racing newspapers are often highlighted. These give the top tips for each daily newspaper. They are usually for short-priced favourites. The bookmakers want the customers to bet on these horses. They know that statistically it is highly unlikely that the favourite will win every race. Favourites lose around 60 per cent of their races. Even on the races they do win, their prices will be small; so, too, will the payouts. Conversely, the bookmaker's profits will be high.

Due to the low prices of the favourites, customers are also more likely to bet on them to win rather than each way. This is also to the bookmaker's advantage as for him, win bets are more profitable than each-way bets.

Betting shops also allow customers to collect their winnings before the weigh-in. This is to ensure that you have your money in time to place a bet on the next race. Even if there is an amended result, the disadvantage to the bookmaker is far outweighed by the speed at which the money is rebet.

Ground

A good time to bet is when the ground has dried out towards the end of the flat season. The form is also more established, which means you have more information about the current season on which to base your selections. You need to bear in mind that some grounds dry out in an irregular way which could give horses on the dryer ground an advantage.

Type of race

The type of race will have an influence on whether or not it is worthwhile making a bet. Amateur, apprentice, ladies' and novice races are too unpredictable and best avoided. The top races are too competitive as they attract the best horses. Races where there is a range of runners and experience are better.

With national hunt there is always the danger that your selection could fall or refuse to jump. Trotting races also have their dangers. Horses are disqualified if they trot and are easily boxed in. This makes flat racing the best choice.

Betting on handicap races

Since handicap races are designed to give all horses an equal chance, they are ideal for backing high-priced runners. All the runners have a chance of winning, which means a high-priced runner also stands a good chance. Here the best value bet is each way. Even if your selection fails to win but is placed you will still get a decent return. If there are more than 16 runners, then you will be paid even if your horse comes in fourth. You don't just have to stick to one selection. With four places to contend, you can select four horses, giving yourself four times as many chances of winning. This can be demonstrated as follows.

Example

Suppose you bet £8 win on a horse at 3/1, your returns would be £32. If your selection comes second, third or fourth, you lose.

If, instead, you bet each way on four horses at fairly high prices, for example 25/1, you now have four chances of winning. The stake is the same £8. The best outcome is that one horse will win and the other three are placed. This would give returns of £110. If one horse wins and two are placed, the returns are £95.50. If only one horse is placed the returns are £7.25. This means that the stake is almost recovered.

With handicaps, the statistics point to the fact that around 48 per cent of winners of flat races are one of the top four in the weights and 62 per cent of winners are in the top six in the weights.

However, there are some races where the top weights do not fare well. In the Grand National, for example, horses from the top end of the handicap tend to do poorly.

Number of runners

Too many runners can make the selection of a winner too difficult. The Grand National is great fun to watch, but not to bet on. There are far too many runners and the difficulty of the fences means that only a minority of the horses finish. Too many incidents during the race make it very hard.

Backing favourites

The problem with backing favourites is that only around 40 per cent of favourites win. Favourites also have the lowest price so it means that any returns are not significant. There is also little value in betting each way due to the low price.

Take the best price

If you have done your homework, you will know what a good price is for your horse. If you are betting in a betting shop, always take a price on your selection, particularly if you are betting on fancied horses. Just before the off, the betting is frantic. This can result in the prices of the fancied horses being hugely reduced between the last show and when the starting price is returned.

At the racecourse shop around. Each bookmaker is offering individual odds. Try to get yourself the best deal possible. Do not be afraid to negotiate a better price or terms. You may find that a bookmaker will give a little extra rather than let his competitors have your business.

One way to get a better price is to quote the true odds based on the way the prices have been calculated. The standard range of prices that you see on offer has been derived from a fraction of 100 and rounded down. A price of 6/1 has been calculated from the fraction of 100/16 which works out as 6 1/4/1. This is then rounded down to 6/1. You can try to get a better price from the bookmaker by calling out '50 to 8 Dobbin'. By doing this you increase your returns by £2. The following table gives the fractions for the standard prices and the percentage increase on returns.

Standard price	As a fraction of 100	Odds to one	% increase on returns
3/1	100/33	3⅓	1
6/1	100/16	6¼	4
7/1	100/14	7⅐	2
8/1	100/12	8⅓	4
12/1	100/8	12½	4
14/1	100/7	14²⁄₇	2
16/1	100/6	16⅔	4
33/1	100/3	33⅓	1

If you are betting on a high-priced horse, you may be able to negotiate a bigger price. As the off time for the race gets nearer, there is often a great deal of betting on the lower priced horses whose prices can be drastically reduced. The prices of the other horses should lengthen but often they tend to get forgotten as the bookmaker is focusing all his attention on the fancied horses. If you want to bet on a higher priced horse and its price has not been lengthened, try to negotiate a bigger price.

Making the best bet

The type of bet you make can influence how much money you win. Some bets are more profitable for the punter than others. Some bets are so unprofitable for the punter that they are simply not worth making. By understanding which bets give the best value, a shrewd gambler can drastically reduce the bookmaker's advantage.

Insight

A study by Nottingham University that compared the betting patterns of men and women found that women won more than men. The reasons for this were that women did not take ridiculous risks. Men were more reckless, often betting on long shots. Instead of betting to win, women were more likely to bet each way, which makes for a more profitable bet.

Profitability of bets

Type of bet	Betting shop's advantage (%)
Ante-post	0
Each-way singles at board price	4
Each-way singles at starting price	5
Win singles at board price	6
Win singles at starting price	8
Each-way doubles	8
Win doubles	10
Forecast singles	12
Each-way multiple bets	18
Win multiple bets	23
Forecast doubles	40

Ante-post bets give you the best value for money. Bookmakers consider themselves fortunate if they break even on these bets. Many people are put off betting ante-post because of the risk of losing their stake if a horse is withdrawn. However, this risk is far outweighed by the more favourable odds that are offered.

The larger ante-post bets are often placed by people who have received information. Even though you may not be in a position to glean that information, it's possible to guess it by monitoring price changes. A large drop in price on a horse can be an indication that there has been a big bet on it.

Betting each way

One of the most profitable bets is an each-way single. These give bookmakers a 4 per cent profit. Consider a result where the favourite wins at 2/1 and a horse at 25/1 comes third. A £1 bet on the winner would give a net profit of £1.73, while a £1 each-way bet on the third horse gives a net profit of £3.46 (calculated at 1/5 odds). Instead of trying to select the winner, it can be more profitable to find which horses will be placed. You also have the added bonus that your selection may just win the race. If your 25/1 horse wins the returns will be £29.12.

Different strategies require different bets. If you are backing a high-priced runner, it makes sense to back it each way as you will still get a decent return if it is placed.

PLACE ODDS FOR EACH-WAY BETS

The number of places and the fraction of odds paid for the place bet are determined by the number of runners and the type of race.

Number of runners	Type of race	Number of places	Fraction of win odds
16+	handicap	4	1/4
12–15	handicap	3	1/4
8–15	not applicable	3	1/5
5–7	not applicable	2	1/4
4 or less	not applicable	1 (win only)	both bets win

Insight

In a race with four runners or less it is not possible to bet each-way. If an each-way bet is made the place stakes are put on the horse to win.

Bets to avoid

Bets to avoid making are all multiple bets like yankees, Canadians, heinz and lucky 15. They give bookmakers the biggest profits. The reason for this is that if one horse loses, instead of losing just one bet, you lose several.

Consider a yankee. It is 11 bets in six doubles, four trebles and a fourfold. If you bet on horses A, B, C and D, then your bets are as follows:

> *Doubles: AB, AC, AD, BC, BD and CD.*
> *Trebles: ABC, ABD, ACD and BCD.*
> *Fourfold: ABCD.*

If horse A loses, you have automatically lost seven bets. All you are left with are four bets BC, BD, CD and BCD. If horse B also loses, you have only one bet left – CD.

Alternatively, make a bet like a super heinz and you lose a massive 63 bets if one of your horses loses. This is the reason why multiple bets are so heavily advertised by the betting shops. They are made to look attractive because bonuses are often added if all your selections win. However, these bonuses rarely get paid because the odds of picking out several winners all on the same day and combining them in one bet are very slim. Even if you do achieve this, the small print of the rules often stipulates that bonuses are paid at starting price odds and not at the prices that you may have taken. Some betting shops also substitute non-runners for the favourite. Again, this gives them a bigger profit. Suppose you play a multiple bet that contains doubles. If you have one winner and a non-runner you would be paid the equivalent of a win single. By putting the favourite in the place of the non-runner, the bookmaker has the advantage that the favourite may lose. Favourites lose around 60 per cent of their races, so the bookmaker has a 60 per cent advantage of your bet losing. Even if the favourite wins, its price will be low so the bookmaker will not have to pay out very much.

Placing large bets

If you are unable to go to a racecourse and want to place a large bet, you need to be particularly careful. Betting shops are notorious for refusing to accept bets at the current advertised odds and instead offer you a lower price. They use this tactic as a means of increasing their profits.

Consider what happens if you want to bet £1000 on a horse whose current price is 7/1. You calculate that your returns will be £8000. Your bet will be immediately passed to the shop manager who will phone his head office. The betting chain employs representatives who place bets for them with bookmakers at the racecourse. The head office will contact their representative and ask him what the best price is for the horse you want to back. Suppose 7/1 is the best price on offer.

You may be told that your bet will be accepted but only at odds of 6/1. Now, instead of winning £8000, you will only get £7000.

You have effectively lost £1000. You are not in a position to bargain, since if you go to another shop, the price may be further reduced. You have to decide whether or not you still want to place the bet.

If you agree to accept the reduced odds of 6/1, the on-course representative will be instructed to place £875 on the horse. He will get odds of 7/1 giving him returns of £7000 if the horse wins. He has also managed to make a profit of £125 on the bet as he was able to take advantage of better odds than you. For the price of a phone call the betting shop has cut your winnings by £1000 and made itself a 12½ per cent profit on your stake.

Insight

To overcome the problem of being offered reduced odds, you need to spread your bets around different shops. It's best to bet with different chains of shops as nearby shops of the same chain may contact one another if they are suspicious about your bet because it is just under the limit for hedging. By placing small bets in several shops you will be able to take the advertised odds.

The maximum amount that you can bet will vary with different betting shops. With the big chains, bets up to £200 will usually be accepted without any problems. With small chains, bets under £50 or with returns of less than £1000 will usually be accepted. On major race days like the Cheltenham meeting and the Grand National meeting, the limits are usually doubled so you can get away with placing larger bets.

Betting shops keep their limits for large bets confidential, but it is fairly easy to discover them with a little stealth. Simply write out a large bet on a horse that has the same price as the one you want to bet on. Hand it to the cashier and pretend to be looking for your wallet. If the bet is passed to the manager and he reaches for the phone, you know you have exceeded the limit. If nothing happens, you know you can safely bet on your selection. Whatever the outcome, ask for your slip to be returned as you cannot find your wallet.

You can then write out a slip for your selection, safe in the knowledge that you will not be offered a reduced price.

Big winners

Bookmakers are in the business of making a profit. If you are continually winning large amounts, you are reducing their profit. For this reason they try to discourage people who win a lot. They achieve this by monitoring people who win on a regular basis. All large wins in betting shops are recorded, typically wins of £500 or over are noted, although smaller wins may be noted if you regularly win. After several big wins a situation will arise when all of your bets will be monitored. Every single bet that you place will be recorded. Your total stakes will be compared with your total winnings. The bookmaker will then take a decision based on your results. If he thinks you are winning too much, you may suddenly find that your bets are refused or he may place a limit on them.

If this happens to you, it is useless trying to argue your case. You should simply place your bets with an alternative chain. However, you can guard against this happening by betting in several different shops. If you have several big wins, change to another shop.

Steamers

The price that each horse attains in the betting is determined by the amount of money that has been bet on it. A horse that has the most money bet on it will have the lowest price and will be the favourite. A horse may first appear in the betting as an outsider. If lots of large bets are placed on the horse to win, its price will be drastically reduced. Often gamblers making large bets have information that the horse has a good chance of winning.

In some cases, a horse may be backed down from an outsider to the favourite. Horses whose prices drop in this manner are called steamers.

Betting on steamers involves keeping a close eye on the betting market. Bets are made on outsiders whose prices are quickly falling. You need to spot the steamers as early as possible to achieve the best possible price before it drops too low.

This is where going to a race meeting can make a big difference. You have the advantage of seeing the changes in betting as they take place. In the first 15 minutes of betting the prices can change a lot as the market is formed. In a betting shop you miss out on all this action, as the prices are transmitted much later. You can still find the steamers, but at the racecourse you can spot them earlier and take advantage of a better price.

Collecting winnings

Take advantage of the early payout of winnings by betting shops. Try to collect your winnings as soon as possible. Sometimes it can be several minutes after a race before a stewards' enquiry or objection is announced. As soon as a stewards' enquiry or objection is announced, betting shops will stop paying out. If you manage to collect your winnings before this announcement, you will not have to return them if the result is amended.

Don't throw away losing betting slips until the race has weighed in. The result of a race is not official until the weigh-in is announced. A stewards' enquiry or objection may be called before the weigh-in. Even if your horse was last past the post, there is still a chance that you could have your stake refunded. The entire race may be voided. If you have thrown away your slip you then need to search on the floor. The problem is the floor is likely to be covered in discarded slips, making it difficult to find your own slip. Also, there is always the chance that someone else may find your slip before you and collect on it.

Betting exchanges

The biggest advantage of betting exchanges is the customers decide their own prices. As individuals are betting they don't need to build in a profit to the book like bookmakers do to cover overheads. The prices offered are therefore much better, on average 20 per cent more than with a bookmaker.

GETTING THE BEST PRICES

Assess the market early. Betting early gives you the opportunity to attempt to get better prices before the market is properly established. As more money is bet, the market becomes more competitive. Prices on the fancied horses tend to drop and those on the less fancied horses drift out. The closer to the off a race is, the tighter the prices become. If you bet early, you also have a greater chance of getting a matched bet and the odds you want. Look at the opening show and anticipate price changes. Be wary of drifting ante-post prices.

SHOPPING AROUND

Each betting exchange will have different prices, by monitoring the prices across a number of betting exchanges you can take the best prices. You can also compare betting exchange prices with bookmakers' prices. A bookmaker must balance his book and, if he has too many bets on a particular horse, will offer better prices on the other horses to achieve this balance.

There are many betting exchanges and bookmakers, all offering different prices. You can bet on more than one exchange at a time or with bookmakers. By shopping around you can find the best prices and make combinations of bets. You can hedge bets where you see profit.

To make the calculations easier to perform, you can use an arbitrage calculator. There are a number of these available on the internet.

GETTING THE BEST ODDS

To get the best prices you will need to bet as early as possible before the market has formed and become competitive. The earlier you place your bet the greater the chance of it becoming matched.

Look out for opportunities to hedge your bets. There will be situations that arise where other players make mistakes with their odds.

Act quickly. If you see a good price, you will need to respond quickly to get your bet on before other customers also see the opportunity.

LAYING FAVOURITES

Favourites lose two-thirds of the time. For this reason bookmakers have always liked favourites and encourage people to bet on them. With a betting exchange, you can now take the place of the bookmaker and bet on the favourites to lose. You won't have the 17 per cent advantage that the bookmaker has and the level of commission that you must pay will have an impact on your winnings but by being selective with the favourites you could make a profit.

Suppose a favourite has a price of 1.4: if you were to back £100 for it to win, you would have to risk £100 for the chance to win £40. By laying, you do the opposite, you risk just £40 for the chance to win £100.

If you make lay bets on ten races at this price and the favourites lose 60 per cent of the time, you will bet £600 and lose £160, with a net win of £440 less commission.

BETTING ON OUTSIDERS

Often the prices for outsiders to win are not as good as they should be. This is because most of the betting tends to be on the low-priced fancied horses. Their prices shorten but the prices of the outsiders don't tend to lengthen to the extent that they should. A horse that should be priced at 41 to win may be just 34. Betting the opposite proposition for them to lose therefore offers a better value bet than a win bet. As a betting exchange allows you to bet on horses losing, you can place lay bets on the horses least likely to win.

Although outsiders lose most of the time, it can be risky to lay them due to the high payout that you need to make if the horse should win. One wrong bet can wipe out the profit from many correct bets.

GETTING BETS ON IN TIME

When betting over the internet, make sure you leave enough time for a bet to be processed. With the internet you need to take account of traffic and the time delay for processing information from one computer to another. Although your computer may show that you placed a bet before the off time of a race, due to the time it takes for the information to leave your computer, reach your internet service provider and then to reach the bookmaker's internet service provider and then the bookmaker's computer, your bet may be too late. The time the bet left your computer is not what counts, it is the time that the bookmaker's computer received your bet.

This time delay may also mean that you miss out on the odds that you want. Odds can rapidly change, especially before the off of a race and you need to be quick to place your bet at the desired odds. If you are not fast enough to place your bet, you will miss some odds.

GETTING STARTED WITH A BETTING EXCHANGE

If using a betting exchange is new to you, start out with small stakes until you get used to the concept. Don't forget that lay bets are the opposite proposition to back bets. With back bets you lose just your stake if your horse loses, but with lay bets you pay out the winnings if the horse wins. Take particular care with laying bets as you can easily lose high multiples of stakes, particularly if you start laying all the horses in a race. Although you are acting like a bookmaker, you haven't got the bookmaker's 17 per cent guaranteed profit built into the prices.

Hedging

Hedging a bet is making an additional bet to guarantee a profit. Because a betting exchange allows you back and lay, you are able to take advantage of price changes and ensure you make a profit regardless of the outcome of the race. Suppose you have bet on a horse to win £100 at 20.0 and its price drops down to 8.0. If you then lay £250 at 8.0, you will make a profit of £150 (less commission) regardless of whether the horse wins or loses.

If the horse wins, your back bet, £100 at 20.0, wins giving a return of £2000. The stake is £100 so the profit is £1900. Your lay bet £250 at 8.0 loses and you lose £1750. Your net profit on the two bets is 1900 − 1750 = £150.

If the horse loses, your lay bet £250 at 800 wins giving a return of £250. Your back bet, £100 at 20.0 loses, so you lose your stake of £100. Your net profit on the two bets is £250 − £100 = £150.

You could also hedge just a portion of your bet, for example, you initially back £100 at 20.0, the price drops and you lay just £100 at 8.0. If the horse wins, your win bet, £100 at 20, wins giving a return of £2000. The stake is £100 so the profit is £1900. Your lay bet £100 at 8.0 loses and you lose £700. Your net profit on the two bets is 1900 − 700 = £1200.

If the horse loses, your win bet, £100 at 20.0, loses and you lose your stake of £100. Your lay bet, £100 at 8.0, wins and you win £100. Your net profit on the two bets is zero.

In this situation, you win £1200 if the horse wins and you lose nothing if it loses.

Online bookmakers can go bust, leaving the betters unpaid.

Keep only the minimum that you need to bet in the internet account and clear out any winnings as soon as possible. If your exchange does go bust, your losses will be minimized.

TIME LAGS

Take advantage of time lags. It takes time for the prices from the racecourse to have an effect on the exchange prices. One of the best times to take advantage of price changes is while other races are running. On a Saturday, for example, there may be a race off at 3.30 and another at 3.35. While the 3.30 race is running, most people who have bet on the race will be watching it and will not be concentrating on what is happening to the prices on the 3.35 race. By comparing bookmakers' prices with exchange prices, there may be an opportunity to anticipate price moves and to make your bets while most of the other betters are otherwise occupied.

There are sites on the internet that provide odds comparison services; they show you the prices across a range of bookmakers and exchanges allowing you to spot the firm offering the best price.

Dutching

Dutching is betting on more than one horse in the same race and working out the correct stakes to be placed on each horse so that the same profit is made whichever of the selected horses wins. It is named after Al Capone's accountant 'Dutch' Schultz who invented the system. The system is useful if you judge that several horses have a good chance of winning.

Suppose you wanted to stake a total of £100 on horses with prices of 2, 4, 12 and 33. In order to win the same amount of money no matter which of the four horses wins, you would need to stake

57.89 at 2, 28.95 at 4, 9.65 at 12 and 3.51 at 33. If one of the horses wins then you will win 15.79.

The internet has dutching calculators that enable you to quickly work out what stakes are needed. To manually work out the stakes, the following formulae are used:

Two horses a and b:
A = *stake on a*
B = *stake on b*
P = *profit*
$A = bP/(ab - (a + b))$
$B = aP/(ab - (a + b))$

Three horses a, b and c:
$A = bcP/(abc - (ab + bc + ac))$
$B = acP/(abc - (ab + bc + ac))$
$C = abP/(abc - (ab + bc + ac))$

Four horses a, b, c and d:
$A = bcdP/(abcd - (abc + bcd + cda + dab))$
$B = acdP/(abcd - (abc + bcd + cda + dab))$
$C = abdP/(abcd - (abc + bcd + cda + dab))$
$D = abcP/(abcd - (abc + bcd + cda + dab))$

The denominator is always the same so it only needs to be calculated once. If the denominator ends up as minus figure then dutching is not possible at the odds you have selected.

Example

You want to back three horses with the prices a 4, b 12 and c 33 and want to make a profit of £100.

$A = 12 \times 33 \times 100 / (4 \times 12 \times 33 - (4 \times 12 + 12 \times 33 + 33 \times 4))$
$= 39,600/1008$
$= 39.29$

(Contd)

The stake on a is £39.29.

B = 4 × 33 × 100/1008
  = 13.10

The stake on b is £13.10

C = 4 × 12 × 100/1008
  = 4.76

The stake on c is £4.76.
Total stake = £57.15.

Returns on a £39.29 × 4 = £157.16.
Returns on b £13.10 × 12 = £157.20.
Returns on c £4.76 × 33 = £157.08.

Syndicate betting

A betting syndicate is a group of people who pool their stakes to make bets. You may consider forming a betting syndicate. You need to find a number of people who all want to bet as part of a team. Each person contributes an agreed amount of capital and any winnings are shared between all members.

There are several advantages. You do not have to play for high stakes. You have the opportunity to make a wider range of bets than your capital alone will allow. The work of assessing the horses can be shared between all members.

HOW TO ORGANIZE A SYNDICATE

Only take part in syndicates with people whom you know and trust. Find a number of people whom you see on a regular basis. Family, friends and work colleagues are the most likely choices.

Although a verbal agreement is legally binding, it is worth taking the time to draw up a written agreement that can be relied on if there is a dispute. You may think it sounds like a lot of trouble to go to, but consider the situation that would arise if the syndicate won a lot of money with, for example, an accumulator. Suppose that particular week you had forgotten to pay your contribution. Would you be entitled to a share of the winnings? Without a written agreement covering that eventuality you would have a lot of trouble proving your case. What would happen if someone had dropped out the week before and now insisted that they were still in the syndicate? How could you prove that they had left the syndicate? If you draw up a written agreement it can save on both the expense and the time taken for court proceedings.

WHAT TO INCLUDE IN THE AGREEMENT

You may think of other things to include but the main requirements are as follows:

▶ *date on which the agreement starts*
▶ *when the agreement ends*
▶ *full names and addresses of every member*
▶ *how much each person pays*
▶ *when payments should be made*
▶ *what happens when someone wants to withdraw from the syndicate.*

Instead of having a continuous agreement, it may be better to operate it for a number of weeks. At the end of that period, you can assess if the agreement is working or if it needs to be amended in some way.

Ensure that all members sign and date the agreement and that each person is given a copy. Make sure you have a contact number for all members in the event of something going wrong.

Insist that anyone wanting to withdraw from the agreement should do so in writing. Make sure you keep a copy of the letter in case of future disputes.

10 THINGS TO REMEMBER

1 *Be aware of the rules.*

2 *Learn how to calculate the profit on a book.*

3 *Keep records of your gambling so that you can assess your performance.*

4 *Set a budget.*

5 *Take account of all costs.*

6 *Be aware of signs that your gambling is out of control and seek help if necessary.*

7 *Be aware of the ways that bookmakers try to make you spend more money.*

8 *Shop around for the best price.*

9 *Avoid multiple bets.*

10 *Large bets need to be spread around different bookmakers in order to stop the bookmaker penalizing you on the price.*

7

....

Checking results and calculating winnings

In this chapter you will learn:
- *how to check results*
- *how to calculate winnings*
- *how to solve disputes with bookmakers*
- *how to use a ready reckoner.*

Checking results

Horse racing results are available in many places, including betting shops, newspapers, teletext, the internet, television (if the racing is broadcast), radio and from the telephone racing lines.

Always double-check results the following morning in a good-quality racing newspaper. Some of the daily tabloid newspapers and text services are notorious for printing the wrong results. If there are printing errors in the quality racing newspapers, these are always communicated to the betting shops.

When you check the results be sure to look out for any factors that may affect the settlement of your bet. These include non-runners, dead heats and rule 4 deductions. If betting on unnamed favourites, check for joint or co-favourites. For each-way bets note the number of runners that actually ran and whether or not the race was a handicap. This allows you to work out the place odds that apply.

Check that your selection was a runner. If it did not run you may be entitled to a refund.

Insight

Occasionally a race may be declared void after a stewards' enquiry. If you bet on a void race you will be entitled to a refund. Also a race meeting may have been abandoned resulting in a refund of stakes.

Disputes with bookmakers

Be aware that different firms have different rules, so you should always read these thoroughly before placing bets. Often there are rules stating what will happen if you make a mistake on the betting slip.

Insight

For example if there is just one horse written on the slip it will often be settled as a winner. The fact that you intended to bet each-way will not count.

Take care if placing large bets as the smaller firms tend to have lower maximum payouts.

Always check how many places a firm pays out for each-way and place bets as some are more generous than others.

LATE BETS

Late bets are void. Be aware that the clocks on betting shop tills do not always show the correct time. Betting shops perform time checks by passing a stamped till receipt through a camera at a set time. They therefore know that a particular clock is, for example, three minutes out. You may have a slip printed with a time before the off but this will not count for settling purposes.

ONE EVENT AFFECTING THE OUTCOME OF ANOTHER

Be aware that if the outcome on one bet affects the outcome on another, you will get lower odds. For example if you place an ante-post double on a horse to win the Cheltenham Gold Cup and the Grand National, you will get reduced odds. The bookmaker argues that because the horse won the first race, its odds for winning the second race would be reduced. Even if the cashier puts the ante-post prices on your slip, the bet will be settled at reduced odds. If you want to place this type of bet, it is best to negotiate a price with the bookmaker before, so you know exactly what your returns will be.

INCORRECT ODDS

Be aware that if odds look too good to be true they may be wrong. Bookmakers' rules give them the right to correct errors in the display or transmission of prices. Bookmakers also have the right to correct errors made by their staff.

TELEPHONE BETS

With telephone betting it is the bet details that the operator reads back to you that count, not what you dictated. It is up to you to check that your bet is correct. If your call gets disconnected, it is up to you to reconnect. If you don't, then the bet will stand as dictated if the instructions are clear and acceptable to the bookmaker.

SETTLING DISPUTES

Do not be afraid to query a bet if you think it has been incorrectly settled. Ask the settler to explain the calculations. You should initially try to settle your claim with the local manager. If this fails you should contact the firm's customer service department. If this fails and the bookmaker is a member of IBAS, you can apply for IBAS to settle the dispute.

Call the IBAS number, available 24 hours a day, to request an arbitration form (telephone 0207 529 7670). Complete the form with all relevant evidence, such as copies of bet receipts. If you are betting over the internet, you should print out the bet confirmation screen. On receipt of the form the service manager will, if he considers it appropriate, refer the dispute to the IBAS panel for adjudication. On completion of the panel's adjudication, both parties will be informed in writing of the decision. All bookmakers operating within IBAS are registered with the service and have agreed to abide by an IBAS ruling. Any bookmaker registered who fails to fulfil that commitment will be removed from the register. Ninety-five per cent of UK bookmakers are registered with IBAS. You can check on the IBAS website to find if a bookmaker is registered. Rulings are not enforceable at law.

DISPUTES WITH INTERNET SITES

If a site is government licensed, you can address any complaints about the site to the licensing authority.

If a firm is a member of the Interactive Gaming Council (IGC), it is possible to apply to the IGC for mediation.

DISPUTES WITH SPREAD BETTING FIRMS

Spread betting firms are regulated by the Financial Services Authority (FSA). The FSA gives spread betting customers a certain degree of protection. There are regulations governing how they promote their service. All forms of communication should be clear, fair and not misleading. The firm should make you aware of the risks, which must be explained in the main part of the text and not hidden away in the small print. If they compare their services with other firms' their comparison must be fair and should not create confusion between itself and its competitors. The firm should include contact details in its communications so that you can ask questions or raise concerns.

If you have a complaint against a firm that you think has not been satisfactorily dealt with by the firm, you have access to the Financial Ombudsman Scheme. In addition, if a spread betting firm goes bust, you have access to the Financial Services Compensation Scheme. The FSA website gives details about how to complain (see Taking it further, page 181).

Calculating winnings

It is vitally important that you know how to calculate winnings on your bets. Settlers may have a couple of thousand bets to deal with on a daily basis. Each bet is calculated literally in seconds. Mistakes do occur, so always check your payouts.

WHERE STAKE FITS PRICE

Most of the calculations to settle bets will involve initially working out the returns to a £1 stake on each price. However, if a win single is being calculated and the stake fits the price it may often be easier to settle.

As we have seen, prices comprise two numbers: the number on the left is the amount that will be won if the amount on the right is staked. The stake is also returned.

If the stake is the same as the number on the right of the price then the bet is very easy to settle. Also, if the stake is a multiple of the number on the right, the bet can be easily settled with the minimum of arithmetic.

£1 win @ 7/1
The stake is £1, which is the same as the number on the right of the price. The winnings are therefore the amount on the left of the price, which is £7. The stake is also refunded, so the total returns are 7 + 1 = £8.

£4 win @ 9/2
The stake is £4. This is double the amount on the right of the price. The winnings will therefore be double the amount on the left of the price (2 × 9 = 18). The stake is also refunded, so the total returns are 18 + 4 = £22.

£4 win @ 13/8
The stake is £4. This is half the number on the right of the price, so the winnings will be half the amount on the left of the price (13/2 = £6.50). The stake is also refunded, therefore the total returns are 6.5 + 4 = £10.50.

FINDING RETURNS TO A ONE-UNIT STAKE

This method of settling allows you to work out the returns to any stake unit. Once you know what the returns are to a one-unit stake, you can simply multiply your stake by that amount to find your winnings.

WIN BETS

There are two ways to find the returns to a £1 stake.

Method 1
▶ *Add together the left and right numbers of the price.*
▶ *Divide by the right number of the price.*

Method 2
▶ *Divide the left number by the right number.*
▶ *Add 1.*

Examples

Finding the £1 returns for each of the following prices using Method 1.

8/11	$\dfrac{8 + 11}{11}$	=	$\dfrac{19}{11}$	= 1.7272
11/8	$\dfrac{11 + 8}{8}$	=	$\dfrac{19}{8}$	= 2.375
7/2	$\dfrac{7 + 2}{2}$	=	$\dfrac{9}{2}$	= 4.5
9/4	$\dfrac{9 + 4}{4}$	=	$\dfrac{13}{4}$	= 3.25

SETTLING WIN SINGLES

1 *Find the returns to a £1 stake on the price.*
2 *Multiply by the stake.*

Examples

Using Method 1:

£5 win @ 7/4. Stake = £5.00

1   $\dfrac{7 + 4}{4} = 2.75$

(Contd)

2   2.75 × 5 = 13.75

Returns = £13.75.

Using Method 2:

1 $\dfrac{7}{4} = 17.5$

1.75 + 1 = 2.75

2   2.75 × 5 = 13.75

Returns = £13.75.

£20 win @ 13/8. Stake = £20.00

1   13 + 8 = 21

$\dfrac{21}{8} = 2.625$

2   2.625 × 20 = 52.50

Returns = £52.50.

EACH-WAY SINGLES

Each-way bets are two bets. One bet is for the selection to win, the other is for the selection to be placed. The place part of the bet is calculated at a fraction of the win price. The fractions are 1/4 and 1/5.

The number of runners, and whether or not the race is a handicap, determines at what fraction the place part of the bet is calculated as follows:

▶ *1–4 runners: win only*
▶ *5–7 runners: 1/4 odds*
▶ *8+ runners: 1/5 odds.*

HANDICAP RACES

▶ *12–15 runners: 1/4 odds*
▶ *16+ runners: 1/4 odds.*

ALL UP TO WIN

All up to win is an expression used where an each-way bet
has been put on a race with four runners or fewer. It is not possible
to bet each way on these races so the place stakes are put on
to win.

> ## Example
>
> Ascot 2.30
> Selection A
> £5.00 each way
> Stake = £10.00
>
> If there were four or fewer runners in the race, then the bet would
> be settled as £10 win selection A.

For each-way multiple bets, the place and win parts need to be
calculated separately. Here the £1 return on the place part of the
bet is the same as the win bet. Therefore, calculate the £1 returns
on the win part of the bet and use the same amount for the place
part of the bet in all further calculations.

EACH-WAY WINNERS

If an each-way bet has been placed on a winner, there is a
quick method for calculating the returns. This can only be used
for each-way singles, it does not work for multiples.

Method

1 *Find the returns for a £1 stake on the winning price.*
2 *Deduct 1.*
3 *Multiply by 1.25 for 1/4 odds or by 1.2 for 1/5 odds.*
4 *Add 2.*
5 *Multiply by the unit stake.*

Examples

£2 each-way winner @ 5/2 (1/5 odds). Tax paid. Stake = £4.36

1 £1 @ 5/2 = 3.5
2 3.5 − 1 = 2.5
3 2.5 × 1.2 (1/5 odds) = 3
4 3 + 2 = 5
5 5 × 2 = 10

Returns = £10.00.

£5 each-way winner @ 7/4 (1/4 odds). Stake = £10.00

1 £1 @ 7/4 = 2.75
2 2.75 − 1 = 1.75
3 1.75 × 1.25 (1/4 odds) = 2.1875
4 2.1875 + 2 = 4.1875
5 4.1875 × 5 = 20.9375

Returns = £20.94.

NON-RUNNERS IN DOUBLES

There is often a lot of confusion over the settling of doubles where one selection is a non-runner. A double is a bet on two selections; if the first selection wins, the returns are bet on the second selection. If the first selection is a non-runner, the returns from the first selection are the original stake, so the original stake goes onto the second selection.

Insight

Many punters incorrectly calculate that they are entitled to a refund of the stakes on the non-runner plus the winnings on the other selection – giving returns of £4. However as shown the refund of the stakes on the first selection becomes the stake for the second selection - giving returns of £3.

Using a ready reckoner

Using a ready reckoner is an easy way of calculating the winnings on your bets. The prices are listed numerically with the lowest price first. There are four columns in each table: the first column gives the stake, the second the win returns, the third the place returns at 1/5 odds and the fourth the place returns at 1/4 odds.

To settle bets:

1 *Find the price of each selection in the tables.*
2 *Find the stake and read across the amount in the appropriate column. For some stakes not shown, it may be necessary to*

add together the amounts in different columns. For example, the stake for £15 is not given, therefore it would be necessary to look up the stakes for £10 and £5 and add them together.

Examples

£5 win @ 7/4. Stake = £5.45.
Find the stake, in this case £5, and read off the amount in the win column = £13.75.
Returns = £13.75

Winner £3 each way @ 13/2 (1/4 odds). Stake = £6.00.
Find the table for 13/2.
Find £3 and read off the amount in the win column = £22.50.
Read off the amount for 1/4 odds = £7.87.
Add both returns 22.50 + 7.87 = 30.375.
Returns = £30.38

£10 win double 11/8 and 8/13. Stake = £10.90.
Find the table for 11/8.
Find the stake of £10 and read off the amount in the win column = £23.75.
As the bet is a double, all the returns from the first selection go onto the second selection.
Find the table for 8/13. The stake is £23.75. As this stake is not in the table, look up the amount for £10 and double it.
Find the amounts for £3, 50p, 20p and 5p.
Total all the individual amounts: 32.30 + 4.84 + 0.80 + 0.32 + 0.08 = 38.34.
Returns = £38.34

10 THINGS TO REMEMBER

1   *Check results with a reputable source.*

2   *Look out for non-runners.*

3   *Be aware of how to solve disputes with bookmakers.*

4   *Learn how to calculate returns to a one unit stake.*

5   *Learn how to calculate your winnings.*

6   *Use a ready reckoner to help you easily calculate winnings.*

7   *Be aware of factors that will affect returns like non runners, dead heats and rule 4 deductions.*

8   *Bookmakers have the right to correct errors in the display or transmission of prices.*

9   *If the outcome on one bet affects the outcome on another you will get lower odds.*

10   *Late bets are void.*

Appendix 1: Ready reckoner

Price Stake	Win	2/7 1/5 odds	1/4 odds	Win	1/3 1/5 odds	1/4 odds	Win	4/11 1/5 odds	1/4 odds	Win	2/5 1/5 odds	1/4 odds	Price Stake
5p	0.06	0.05	0.05	0.06	0.10	0.05	0.06	0.05	0.05	0.07	0.05	0.05	5p
10p	0.12	0.10	0.10	0.13	0.10	0.10	0.13	0.10	0.10	0.14	0.10	0.11	10p
20p	0.25	0.21	0.21	0.26	0.21	0.21	0.27	0.21	0.21	0.28	0.21	0.22	20p
50p	0.64	0.54	0.53	0.66	0.53	0.54	0.68	0.53	0.54	0.70	0.54	0.55	50p
£1	1.28	1.05	1.07	1.33	1.06	1.08	1.36	1.07	1.09	1.40	1.08	1.10	£1
£2	2.56	2.11	2.14	2.66	2.13	2.16	2.72	2.14	2.18	2.80	2.16	2.20	£2
£3	3.85	3.17	3.21	4.00	3.19	3.25	4.09	3.21	3.27	4.20	3.24	3.30	£3
£4	5.14	4.22	4.28	5.33	4.26	4.33	5.45	4.29	4.36	5.60	4.32	4.40	£4
£5	6.42	5.28	5.35	6.66	5.33	5.41	6.81	5.36	5.45	7.00	5.40	5.50	£5
£6	7.71	6.34	6.42	8.00	6.40	6.50	8.18	6.43	6.54	8.40	6.48	6.60	£6
£7	9.00	7.40	7.50	9.33	7.46	7.58	9.54	7.50	7.63	9.80	7.56	7.70	£7
£8	10.28	8.45	8.57	10.66	8.53	8.66	10.90	8.58	8.72	11.20	8.64	8.80	£8
£9	11.57	9.51	9.64	12.00	9.60	9.75	12.27	9.65	9.81	12.60	9.72	9.90	£9
£10	12.85	10.57	10.71	13.33	10.66	10.83	13.63	10.72	10.90	14.00	10.80	11.00	£10

Price Stake	4/9 Win	1/5 odds	1/4 odds	40/85 Win	1/5 odds	1/4 odds	1/2 Win	1/5 odds	1/4 odds	8/15 Win	1/5 odds	1/4 odds	Price Stake
5p	0.07	0.10	0.11	0.07	0.05	0.05	0.07	0.05	0.05	0.07	0.05	0.05	5p
10p	0.14	0.10	0.11	0.14	0.10	0.11	0.15	0.11	0.11	0.15	0.11	0.11	10p
20p	0.28	0.21	0.22	0.29	0.21	0.22	0.30	0.22	0.22	0.30	0.22	0.22	20p
50p	0.72	0.54	0.55	0.73	0.54	0.55	0.75	0.55	0.56	0.76	0.55	0.56	50p
£1	1.44	1.08	1.11	1.47	1.09	1.11	1.50	1.10	1.12	1.53	1.10	1.13	£1
£2	2.88	2.17	2.22	2.94	2.18	2.23	3.00	2.20	2.25	3.06	2.21	2.26	£2
£3	4.33	3.26	3.33	4.41	3.28	3.35	4.50	3.30	3.37	4.60	3.31	3.40	£3
£4	5.77	4.35	4.44	5.88	4.37	4.47	6.00	4.40	5.06	6.13	4.42	4.53	£4
£5	7.22	5.44	5.55	7.35	5.47	5.58	7.50	5.50	5.62	7.66	5.53	5.66	£5
£6	8.66	6.53	6.66	8.82	6.56	6.70	9.00	6.60	6.75	9.20	6.64	6.80	£6
£7	10.11	7.62	7.77	10.29	7.65	7.82	10.50	7.70	7.87	10.73	7.74	7.93	£7
£8	11.55	8.71	8.88	11.76	8.75	8.94	12.00	8.80	9.00	12.26	8.85	9.06	£8
£9	13.00	9.79	10.00	13.23	9.84	10.05	13.50	9.90	10.12	13.80	9.96	10.20	£9
£10	14.44	10.88	11.11	14.70	10.94	11.17	15.00	11.00	11.25	15.33	11.06	11.33	£10

Price Stake	4/7			8/13			4/6			8/11			Price Stake
	Win	1/5 odds	1/4 odds	Win	1/5 odds	1/4 odds	Win	1/5 odds	1/4 odds	Win	1/5 odds	1/4 odds	
5p	0.07	0.05	0.05	0.08	0.05	0.05	0.08	0.05	0.05	0.08	0.05	0.05	5p
10p	0.15	0.11	0.11	0.16	0.11	0.11	0.16	0.11	0.11	0.17	0.11	0.11	10p
20p	0.31	0.22	0.22	0.32	0.22	0.23	0.33	0.22	0.23	0.34	0.22	0.23	20p
50p	0.78	0.55	0.57	0.80	0.56	0.57	0.83	0.56	0.58	0.86	0.57	0.59	50p
£1	1.57	1.11	1.14	1.61	1.12	1.15	1.66	1.13	1.16	1.72	1.14	1.18	£1
£2	3.14	2.22	2.28	3.23	2.24	2.30	3.33	2.26	2.33	3.45	2.29	2.36	£2
£3	4.71	3.34	3.42	4.84	3.36	3.46	5.00	3.40	4.08	5.18	3.43	3.54	£3
£4	6.28	4.45	4.57	6.46	4.49	4.61	6.66	4.53	4.66	6.90	4.58	4.72	£4
£5	7.85	5.57	6.40	8.07	5.61	5.76	8.33	5.66	5.83	8.63	5.72	5.90	£5
£6	9.42	6.68	6.85	9.69	6.73	6.92	10.00	6.80	7.00	10.36	6.87	7.09	£6
£7	11.00	7.80	8.00	11.30	7.86	8.07	11.66	7.93	8.16	12.09	8.01	8.27	£7
£8	12.57	8.91	9.14	12.92	8.98	9.23	13.13	9.06	9.33	13.81	9.16	9.45	£8
£9	14.14	10.02	10.28	14.53	10.10	10.38	15.00	10.20	10.50	15.54	10.30	10.63	£9
£10	15.71	11.14	11.42	16.15	11.23	11.53	16.66	11.33	11.66	17.27	11.45	11.81	£10

Price Stake	Win	4/5 1/5 odds	1/4 odds	Win	5/6 1/5 odds	1/4 odds	Win	10/11 1/5 odds	1/4 odds	Win	20/21 1/5 odds	1/4 odds	Price Stake
5p	0.09	0.05	0.06	0.09	0.05	0.06	0.09	0.05	0.06	0.09	0.05	0.06	5p
10p	0.18	0.11	0.12	0.18	0.11	0.12	0.19	0.11	0.12	0.19	0.11	0.12	10p
20p	0.36	0.23	0.24	0.36	0.23	0.24	0.38	0.23	0.24	0.39	0.23	0.24	20p
50p	0.90	0.58	0.60	0.91	0.58	0.60	0.95	0.59	0.61	0.97	0.59	0.61	50p
£1	1.80	1.16	1.20	1.83	1.16	1.20	1.90	1.18	1.22	1.95	1.19	1.23	£1
£2	3.60	2.32	2.40	3.66	2.33	2.41	3.81	2.36	2.45	3.90	2.38	2.47	£2
£3	5.40	3.48	3.60	5.50	3.50	3.62	5.72	3.54	3.68	5.85	3.57	3.71	£3
£4	7.20	4.64	4.80	7.33	4.66	4.83	7.63	4.72	4.90	7.80	4.76	4.95	£4
£5	9.00	5.80	6.00	9.16	5.83	6.04	9.54	5.90	6.13	9.76	5.95	6.19	£5
£6	10.80	6.96	7.20	11.00	7.00	7.25	11.45	7.09	7.36	11.71	7.14	7.42	£6
£7	12.60	8.12	8.40	12.83	8.16	8.45	13.36	8.27	8.59	13.66	8.33	8.66	£7
£8	14.40	9.28	9.60	14.66	9.33	9.66	15.27	9.45	9.81	15.61	9.52	9.90	£8
£9	16.20	10.44	10.80	16.50	10.49	10.87	17.18	10.63	11.04	17.57	10.71	11.14	£9
£10	18.00	11.60	12.00	18.33	11.66	12.08	19.09	11.81	12.27	19.52	11.90	12.38	£10

Price Stake	Evens 1/1 Win	1/5 odds	1/4 odds	21/20 Win	1/5 odds	1/4 odds	11/10 Win	1/5 odds	1/4 odds	6/5 Win	1/5 odds	1/4 odds	Price Stake
5p	0.10	0.06	0.06	0.10	0.06	0.06	0.10	0.06	0.06	0.11	0.06	0.06	5p
10p	0.20	0.12	0.12	0.20	0.12	0.12	0.21	0.12	0.12	0.22	0.12	0.13	10p
20p	0.40	0.24	0.25	0.41	0.24	0.25	0.42	0.24	0.25	0.44	0.24	0.26	20p
50p	1.00	0.60	0.62	1.02	0.60	0.63	1.05	0.61	0.63	1.10	0.62	0.65	50p
£1	2.00	1.20	1.25	2.05	1.21	1.26	2.10	1.22	1.27	2.20	1.24	1.30	£1
£2	4.00	2.40	2.50	4.10	2.42	2.52	4.20	2.44	2.55	4.40	2.48	2.60	£2
£3	6.00	3.60	3.75	6.15	3.63	3.78	6.30	3.66	3.82	6.60	4.72	3.90	£3
£4	8.00	4.80	5.00	8.20	4.84	5.05	8.40	4.88	5.10	8.80	5.96	5.20	£4
£5	10.00	6.00	6.25	10.25	6.05	6.31	10.50	6.10	6.37	11.00	6.20	6.50	£5
£6	12.00	7.20	7.50	12.30	7.26	7.57	12.60	7.32	7.65	13.20	7.44	7.80	£6
£7	14.00	8.40	8.75	14.35	8.37	8.83	14.70	8.54	8.92	14.40	8.68	9.10	£7
£8	16.00	9.60	10.00	16.40	9.58	10.10	16.80	9.76	10.20	16.60	9.92	10.40	£8
£9	18.00	10.80	11.25	18.45	10.79	11.36	18.90	10.98	11.47	18.80	11.16	11.70	£9
£10	20.00	12.00	12.50	20.50	12.10	12.62	21.00	12.20	12.75	22.00	12.40	13.00	£10

Price/Stake	5/4 1/5 odds	5/4 1/4 odds	5/4 Win	11/8 1/5 odds	11/8 1/4 odds	11/8 Win	6/4 1/5 odds	6/4 1/4 odds	6/4 Win	13/8 1/5 odds	13/8 1/4 odds	13/8 Win	Price/Stake
5p	0.06	0.06	0.11	0.06	0.06	0.11	0.06	0.06	0.12	0.06	0.07	0.13	5p
10p	0.12	0.13	0.22	0.12	0.13	0.23	0.13	0.13	0.25	0.13	0.14	0.26	10p
20p	0.25	0.26	0.44	0.25	0.26	0.47	0.26	0.27	0.50	0.26	0.28	0.52	20p
50p	0.62	0.65	1.12	0.63	0.67	1.18	0.65	0.68	1.25	0.66	0.70	1.31	50p
£1	1.25	1.31	2.25	1.27	1.34	2.37	1.30	1.37	2.50	1.32	1.40	2.62	£1
£2	2.50	2.62	4.50	2.55	2.68	4.75	2.60	2.75	5.00	2.65	2.81	5.25	£2
£3	3.75	3.93	6.75	3.82	4.03	7.12	3.90	4.12	7.50	3.97	4.21	7.87	£3
£4	5.00	5.25	9.00	5.10	5.37	9.50	5.20	5.50	10.00	5.30	5.62	10.50	£4
£5	6.25	6.56	11.25	6.37	6.71	11.87	6.50	6.87	12.50	6.62	7.03	13.12	£5
£6	7.50	7.87	13.50	7.65	8.06	14.25	7.80	8.25	15.00	7.95	8.43	15.75	£6
£7	8.75	9.18	15.75	8.92	9.40	16.62	9.10	9.62	17.50	9.27	9.84	18.37	£7
£8	10.00	10.50	18.00	10.20	10.75	19.00	10.40	11.00	20.00	10.60	11.25	21.00	£8
£9	11.25	11.81	20.25	11.47	12.09	21.37	11.70	12.37	22.50	11.92	12.65	23.62	£9
£10	12.50	13.12	22.50	12.75	13.43	23.75	13.00	13.75	25.00	13.25	14.06	26.25	£10

Price Stake	7/4 Win	1/5 odds	1/4 odds	15/8 Win	1/5 odds	1/4 odds	2/1 Win	1/5 odds	1/4 odds	85/40 Win	1/5 odds	1/4 odds	Price Stake
5p	0.13	0.06	0.07	0.14	0.06	0.07	0.15	0.07	0.07	0.15	0.07	0.07	5p
10p	0.27	0.13	0.14	0.28	0.13	0.14	0.30	0.14	0.15	0.31	0.14	0.15	10p
20p	0.55	0.27	0.28	0.57	0.27	0.29	0.60	0.28	0.30	0.62	0.28	0.30	20p
50p	1.37	0.67	0.71	1.43	0.68	0.73	1.50	0.70	0.75	1.56	0.71	0.76	50p
£1	2.75	1.35	1.43	2.87	1.37	1.46	3.00	1.40	1.50	3.12	1.42	1.53	£1
£2	5.50	2.70	2.87	5.75	2.75	2.93	6.00	2.80	3.00	6.25	2.85	3.06	£2
£3	8.25	4.05	4.31	8.62	4.12	4.40	9.00	4.20	4.50	9.37	4.27	4.59	£3
£4	11.00	5.40	5.75	11.50	5.50	5.87	12.00	5.60	6.00	12.50	5.70	6.12	£4
£5	13.75	6.75	7.18	14.37	6.87	7.34	15.00	7.00	7.50	15.62	7.12	7.65	£5
£6	16.50	8.10	8.62	17.25	8.25	8.81	18.00	8.40	9.00	18.75	8.55	9.18	£6
£7	19.25	9.45	10.06	20.12	9.62	10.28	21.00	9.80	10.50	21.87	9.97	10.71	£7
£8	22.00	10.80	11.50	23.00	11.00	11.75	24.00	11.20	12.00	25.00	11.40	12.25	£8
£9	24.75	12.15	12.93	25.87	12.37	13.21	27.00	12.60	13.50	28.12	12.82	13.78	£9
£10	27.50	13.50	14.36	28.75	13.75	14.68	30.00	14.00	15.00	31.25	14.25	15.31	£10

Price Stake	9/4 Win	9/4 1/5 odds	9/4 1/4 odds	5/2 Win	5/2 1/5 odds	5/2 1/4 odds	11/4 Win	11/4 1/5 odds	11/4 1/4 odds	3/1 Win	3/1 1/5 odds	3/1 1/4 odds	Price Stake
5p	0.16	0.07	0.07	0.17	0.07	0.08	0.18	0.07	0.08	0.20	0.08	0.08	5p
10p	0.32	0.14	0.15	0.35	0.15	0.16	0.37	0.15	0.16	0.40	0.16	0.17	10p
20p	0.65	0.29	0.31	0.70	0.30	0.32	0.75	0.31	0.33	0.80	0.32	0.35	20p
50p	1.72	0.72	0.78	1.75	0.75	0.81	1.87	0.77	0.84	2.00	0.80	0.87	50p
£1	3.25	1.45	1.56	3.50	1.50	1.62	3.75	1.55	1.68	4.00	1.60	1.75	£1
£2	6.50	2.90	3.12	7.00	3.00	3.25	7.50	3.10	3.37	8.00	3.20	3.50	£2
£3	9.75	4.35	4.68	10.50	4.50	4.87	11.25	4.65	5.06	12.00	4.80	5.25	£3
£4	13.00	5.80	6.25	14.00	6.00	6.50	15.00	6.20	6.75	16.00	6.40	7.00	£4
£5	16.25	7.25	7.81	17.50	7.50	8.12	18.75	7.75	8.43	20.00	8.00	8.75	£5
£6	19.50	3.70	9.37	21.00	9.00	9.75	22.50	9.30	10.12	24.00	9.60	10.50	£6
£7	22.75	10.15	10.93	24.50	10.50	11.37	26.25	10.85	11.81	28.00	11.20	12.25	£7
£8	26.00	11.60	12.50	28.00	12.00	13.00	30.00	12.40	13.50	32.00	12.80	14.00	£8
£9	29.25	13.05	14.06	31.50	13.50	14.62	33.75	13.95	15.18	36.00	14.40	15.75	£9
£10	32.50	14.50	15.62	35.00	15.00	16.25	37.50	15.50	16.87	40.00	16.00	17.50	£10

Price Stake	100/30, 10/3 Win	1/5 odds	1/4 odds	7/2 Win	1/5 odds	1/4 odds	4/1 Win	1/5 odds	1/4 odds	9/2 Win	1/5 odds	1/4 odds	Price Stake
5p	0.21	0.08	0.09	0.22	0.08	0.09	0.25	0.09	0.10	0.27	0.09	0.10	5p
10p	0.43	0.16	0.18	0.45	0.17	0.18	0.50	0.18	0.20	0.55	0.19	0.21	10p
20p	0.86	0.33	0.36	0.90	0.34	0.37	1.00	0.36	0.40	1.10	0.38	0.42	20p
50p	2.16	0.83	0.91	2.25	0.85	0.93	2.50	0.90	1.00	2.75	0.95	1.06	50p
£1	4.33	1.66	1.83	4.50	1.70	1.87	5.00	1.80	2.00	5.50	1.90	2.12	£1
£2	8.66	3.33	3.66	9.00	3.40	3.75	10.00	3.60	4.00	11.00	3.80	4.25	£2
£3	13.00	5.00	5.50	13.50	5.10	5.62	15.00	5.40	6.00	16.50	5.70	6.37	£3
£4	17.33	6.66	7.33	18.00	6.80	7.50	20.00	7.20	8.00	22.00	7.60	8.50	£4
£5	21.66	8.33	9.16	22.50	8.50	9.37	25.00	9.00	10.00	27.50	9.50	10.62	£5
£6	26.00	10.00	11.00	27.00	10.20	11.25	30.00	10.80	12.00	33.00	11.40	12.75	£6
£7	30.33	11.66	12.83	31.50	11.90	13.12	35.00	12.60	14.00	38.50	13.30	14.87	£7
£8	34.66	13.33	14.66	36.00	13.60	15.00	40.00	14.40	16.00	44.00	15.20	17.00	£8
£9	39.00	15.00	16.50	40.50	15.30	16.87	45.00	16.20	18.00	49.50	17.10	19.12	£9
£10	43.33	16.66	18.33	45.00	17.00	18.75	50.00	18.00	20.00	55.00	19.00	21.25	£10

Price Stake	5/1 Win	5/1 1/5 odds	5/1 1/4 odds	11/2 Win	11/2 1/5 odds	11/2 1/4 odds	6/1 Win	6/1 1/5 odds	6/1 1/4 odds	13/2 Win	13/2 1/5 odds	13/2 1/4 odds	Price Stake
5P	0.30	0.10	0.11	0.32	0.10	0.11	0.35	0.11	0.12	0.37	0.11	0.13	5P
10P	0.60	0.20	0.22	0.65	0.21	0.23	0.70	0.22	0.25	0.75	0.23	0.26	10P
20P	1.20	0.40	0.45	1.30	0.42	0.47	1.40	0.44	0.50	1.50	0.46	0.53	20P
50P	3.00	1.00	1.12	3.25	1.05	1.18	3.50	1.10	1.25	3.75	1.15	1.31	50P
£1	6.00	2.00	2.25	6.50	2.10	2.37	7.00	2.20	2.50	7.50	2.30	2.62	£1
£2	12.00	4.00	4.50	13.00	4.20	4.75	14.00	4.40	5.00	15.00	4.60	5.25	£2
£3	18.00	6.00	6.75	19.50	6.30	7.12	21.00	6.60	7.50	22.50	6.90	7.87	£3
£4	24.00	8.00	9.00	26.00	8.40	9.50	28.00	8.80	10.00	30.00	9.20	10.50	£4
£5	30.00	10.00	11.25	32.50	10.50	11.87	35.00	11.00	12.50	37.50	11.50	13.12	£5
£6	36.00	12.00	13.50	39.00	12.60	14.25	42.00	13.20	15.00	45.00	13.80	15.75	£6
£7	42.00	14.00	15.75	45.50	14.70	16.62	49.00	15.40	17.50	52.50	16.10	18.37	£7
£8	48.00	16.00	18.00	52.00	16.80	19.00	56.00	17.60	20.00	60.00	18.40	21.00	£8
£9	54.00	18.00	20.25	58.50	18.90	21.37	63.00	19.80	22.50	67.50	20.70	23.62	£9
£10	60.00	20.00	22.50	65.00	21.00	23.75	70.00	22.00	25.00	75.00	23.00	26.25	£10

Price Stake	7/1 Win	7/1 1/5 odds	7/1 1/4 odds	15/2 Win	15/2 1/5 odds	15/2 1/4 odds	8/1 Win	8/1 1/5 odds	8/1 1/4 odds	17/2 Win	17/2 1/5 odds	17/2 1/4 odds	Price Stake
5p	0.40	0.12	0.13	0.42	0.12	0.14	0.45	0.13	0.15	0.47	0.13	0.15	5p
10p	0.80	0.24	0.27	0.85	0.25	0.28	0.90	0.26	0.30	0.95	0.27	0.31	10p
20p	1.60	0.48	0.55	1.70	0.50	0.57	1.80	0.52	0.60	1.90	0.54	0.62	20p
50p	4.00	1.20	1.37	4.25	1.25	1.43	4.50	1.30	1.50	4.75	1.35	1.56	50p
£1	8.00	2.40	2.75	8.50	2.50	2.87	9.00	2.60	3.00	9.50	2.70	3.12	£1
£2	16.00	4.80	5.50	17.00	5.00	5.75	18.00	5.20	6.00	19.00	5.40	6.25	£2
£3	24.00	7.20	8.25	25.50	7.50	8.62	27.00	7.80	9.00	28.50	8.10	9.37	£3
£4	32.00	9.60	11.00	34.00	10.00	11.50	36.00	10.40	12.00	38.00	10.80	12.50	£4
£5	40.00	12.00	13.75	42.50	12.50	14.37	45.00	13.00	15.00	47.50	13.50	15.62	£5
£6	48.00	14.40	16.50	51.00	15.00	17.25	54.00	15.60	18.00	57.00	16.20	18.75	£6
£7	56.00	16.80	19.25	59.50	17.50	20.12	63.00	18.20	21.00	66.50	18.90	21.87	£7
£8	64.00	19.20	22.00	68.00	20.00	23.00	72.00	20.80	24.00	76.00	21.60	25.00	£8
£9	72.00	21.60	24.75	75.50	22.50	25.87	81.00	23.40	27.00	85.50	24.30	28.12	£9
£10	80.00	24.00	27.50	85.00	25.00	28.75	90.00	26.00	30.00	95.00	27.00	31.25	£10

Price Stake	9/1			10/1			11/1			12/1			Price Stake
	Win	1/5 odds	1/4 odds	Win	1/5 odds	1/4 odds	Win	1/5 odds	1/4 odds	Win	1/5 odds	1/4 odds	
5p	0.50	0.14	0.16	0.55	0.15	0.17	0.60	0.16	0.18	0.65	0.17	0.20	5p
10p	1.00	0.28	0.32	1.10	0.30	0.35	1.20	0.32	0.37	1.30	0.34	0.40	10p
20p	2.00	0.56	0.65	2.20	0.60	0.70	2.40	0.64	0.75	2.60	0.68	0.80	20p
50p	5.00	1.40	1.62	5.50	1.50	1.75	6.00	1.60	1.87	6.50	1.70	2.00	50p
£1	10.00	2.80	3.25	11.00	3.00	3.50	12.00	3.20	3.75	13.00	3.40	4.00	£1
£2	20.00	5.60	6.50	22.00	6.00	7.00	24.00	6.40	7.50	26.00	6.80	8.00	£2
£3	30.00	8.40	9.75	33.00	9.00	10.50	36.00	9.60	11.25	39.00	10.20	12.00	£3
£4	40.00	11.20	13.00	44.00	12.00	14.00	48.00	12.80	15.00	52.00	13.60	16.00	£4
£5	50.00	14.00	16.25	55.00	15.00	17.50	60.00	16.00	18.75	65.00	17.00	20.00	£5
£6	60.00	16.80	19.50	66.00	18.00	21.00	72.00	19.20	22.50	78.00	20.40	24.00	£6
£7	70.00	19.60	22.75	77.00	21.00	24.50	84.00	22.40	26.25	91.00	23.80	28.00	£7
£8	80.00	22.40	26.00	88.00	24.00	28.00	96.00	25.60	30.00	104.00	27.20	32.00	£8
£9	90.00	25.20	29.25	99.00	27.00	31.50	108.00	28.80	33.75	117.00	30.60	36.00	£9
£10	100.00	28.00	32.50	110.00	30.00	35.00	120.00	32.00	37.50	130.00	34.00	40.00	£10

Price Stake	14/1 Win	1/5 odds	1/4 odds	16/1 Win	1/5 odds	1/4 odds	20/1 Win	1/5 odds	1/4 odds	25/1 Win	1/5 odds	1/4 odds	33/1 Win	1/5 odds	1/4 odds
5p	0.75	0.16	0.22	0.85	0.21	0.25	1.05	0.25	0.30	1.30	0.30	0.36	1.70	0.39	0.46
10p	1.50	0.38	0.45	1.70	0.42	0.50	2.10	0.50	0.60	2.60	0.60	0.72	3.40	0.76	0.92
20p	3.00	0.76	0.90	3.40	0.84	1.00	4.20	1.00	1.20	5.20	1.20	1.45	6.80	1.52	1.85
50p	7.50	1.90	2.25	8.50	2.10	2.50	10.50	2.50	3.00	13.00	3.00	3.62	17.00	3.80	4.62
£1	15.00	3.80	4.50	17.00	4.20	5.00	21.00	5.00	6.00	26.00	6.00	7.25	34.00	7.60	9.25
£2	30.00	7.60	9.00	34.00	8.40	10.00	42.00	10.00	12.00	52.00	12.00	14.50	68.00	15.20	18.50
£3	45.00	11.40	13.50	51.00	12.60	15.00	63.00	15.00	18.00	65.00	18.00	21.75	102.00	22.80	27.75
£4	60.00	15.20	18.00	68.00	16.80	20.00	84.00	20.00	24.00	104.00	24.00	29.00	136.00	30.40	37.00
£5	75.00	19.00	22.50	85.00	21.00	25.00	105.00	25.00	30.00	130.00	30.00	36.25	170.00	38.00	46.25
£6	90.00	22.80	27.00	102.00	25.20	30.00	126.00	30.00	36.00	156.00	36.00	43.50	204.00	45.60	55.50
£7	105.00	26.60	31.50	119.00	29.40	35.00	147.00	35.00	42.00	182.00	42.00	50.75	238.00	53.20	64.75
£8	120.00	30.40	36.00	136.00	33.60	40.00	168.00	40.00	48.00	208.00	48.00	58.00	272.00	60.80	74.00
£9	135.00	34.20	40.50	153.00	37.80	45.00	189.00	45.00	54.00	234.00	54.00	65.25	306.00	68.40	83.25
£10	150.00	38.00	45.00	170.00	42.00	50.00	210.00	50.00	60.00	260.00	60.00	72.50	340.00	76.00	92.50

Price Stake	40/1 Win	1/5 odds	1/4 odds	50/1 Win	1/5 odds	1/4 odds	66/1 Win	1/5 odds	1/4 odds	100/1 Win	1/5 odds	1/4 odds
5p	2.05	0.45	0.55	2.55	0.55	0.67	3.35	0.71	0.87	5.05	1.05	1.30
10p	4.10	0.90	1.10	5.10	1.10	1.35	6.70	1.42	1.75	10.10	2.10	2.60
20p	8.20	1.80	2.20	10.20	2.20	2.70	13.40	2.84	3.50	20.20	4.20	5.20
50p	20.50	4.50	5.50	25.50	5.50	6.75	33.50	7.10	8.75	50.50	10.50	13.00
£1	41.00	9.00	11.00	51.00	11.00	13.50	67.00	14.20	17.50	101.00	21.00	26.00
£2	82.00	18.00	22.00	102.00	22.00	27.00	134.00	28.40	35.00	202.00	42.00	52.00
£3	123.00	27.00	33.00	153.00	33.00	40.50	201.00	42.60	52.50	303.00	63.00	78.00
£4	164.00	36.00	44.00	204.00	44.00	54.00	268.00	56.80	70.00	404.00	84.00	104.00
£5	205.00	45.00	55.00	255.00	55.00	67.50	335.00	71.00	87.50	505.00	105.00	130.00
£6	246.00	54.00	66.00	306.00	66.00	81.00	402.00	85.20	105.00	606.00	126.00	156.00
£7	287.00	63.00	77.00	357.00	77.00	94.50	469.00	99.40	122.50	707.00	147.00	182.00
£8	328.00	72.00	88.00	408.00	88.00	108.00	536.00	113.60	140.00	808.00	168.00	208.00
£9	369.00	81.00	99.00	459.00	99.00	121.50	603.00	127.80	157.50	909.00	189.00	234.00
£10	410.00	90.00	110.00	510.00	110.00	135.00	670.00	142.00	175.00	1010.00	210.00	260.00

Appendix 2: Jargon guide

abandoned racing has been called off at that particular meeting

accumulator a bet on any number of selections, in different races, where the winnings on the first horse go onto the second and then onto the third and then onto the fourth and so on

allowance weight conceded by professional jockeys to apprentices or conditional to compensate for their inexperience

also-ran a horse that lost

apprentice a young jockey tied by contract to a trainer while learning flat racing

arbitrage back and lay or buy and sell in the same market to make a profit

awt all-weather fibre-sand track

back bet that a horse will win

back all bet that all the horses in a race will win

banker a horse that is strongly fancied and is often the main selection in multiple bets

board price current price on offer for a horse

book percentage figure that shows the profit of a book. The book percentage minus 100 gives the percentage profit or loss that is made by betting on all runners. A figure greater than 100 is its profit. The percentage less than 100 is the percentage loss on a book

bookies betting shop or bookmakers

boxed in when a horse cannot overtake another because one or more horses block its path

brought down a horse that has fallen due to the actions of another horse

bumper a flat race for horses bred for national hunt

burlington bertie a price of 100/30

carpet a price of 3/1

clerk of the course racecourse official who manages the race day

clerk of the scales Jockey Club official who ensures horses carry the correct weight

closing a bet (spread betting) placing a second bet of the same size in the opposite direction of the initial bet

co-favourites where there are more than two favourites

colours silk shirts worn by the jockey

colt young male horse, aged 4 years and under

commission amount charged for services supplied by a betting exchange or spread betting firm

conditional young jockey tied by contract to a trainer while learning national hunt racing

conditions race a race where horses carry weight according to factors such as age, sex, whether they have won before or the type of race won

connections people allied with a horse, such as the trainer and owner

dead heat where a race is a tie for either the winner or one of the placed horses

decimal odds odds where the stake is included in the price, for example 2/1 is 3.0

double carpet a price of 33/1

down bet a bet that the result will be lower than the lower end of the quote. Also called a sell

draw the position of a horse in the starting stalls

drift odds that lengthen

dutching betting different stakes on several horses in a race to give the same payout no matter which of the selections wins

dwelt slow at the start

evens a price of 1/1

faces bookmakers' slang for punters with inside information about horses

favourite the horse with the lowest price

fc forecast

field runners in a race

filly a female horse up to 4 years old

first time out a horse running in its first race

form a record of a horse's previous racing performance

furlong an eighth of a mile (201 metres)

gelding a castrated male horse

gentleman jockey an amateur jockey

going condition of the racing surface

going down horses are on their way to the start

grand £1000

green a description of an inexperienced horse

hand a measure of a horse's height, equivalent to four inches

hedge place additional bets to guarantee a profit

home stretch length of straight track before the finishing post

IBAS the Independent Betting Arbitration Service, a British organization that settles disputes with bookmakers on punters' behalf when the bookmaker is a member of the scheme

in running betting on an event as it happens

in the money a horse that wins or is placed

index bet a bet where the performance is measured by awarding points for a particular outcome

inspection due either to the weather or condition of the course, a decision will be made about whether or not racing can go ahead

irons stirrups

joint favourites two horses are favourite

jolly the favourite

judge Jockey Club official who declares the race result and the distances between runners

juvenile a 2-year-old horse in flat racing, a 3- or 4-year-old horse in jump racing

lame a horse that is having difficulty walking or is limping

lay bet that a horse will lose

lay all bet that all the horses in a race will lose

layers bookmakers

laying off bookmakers' practice of reducing betting liability by betting with other bookmakers

long shot a horse with high odds

maiden a horse or rider that has not previously won a race

makeup result on which a bet is settled

mare female horse aged 5 years and over

match a race in which there are only two horses competing

maximum makeup a maximum limit on the result

monkey £500

nap top tip of the day from a racing tipster

no offers no price is offered by the bookmakers. N/O is
displayed on the board

novice a jump racing term: a novice hurdler is a horse that has
not won a hurdle race before the current season; a novice
chaser is a horse that has not won a steeplechase before the
current season

objection a complaint from a jockey that, in his opinion, the
rules of racing have been broken

odds on a price lower than evens

off the race has started

open bet a bet that has not been closed or settled

outsider a horse with little chance of winning

over-round profit on a book

pacer a horse in harness racing that moves its legs on one side
of its body in unison

pari-mutuel prices quoted by the French tote

pattern created in 1971 to ensure that the major European
races are spread out across the season and do not clash.
Pattern races are classified in groups one to three with Group
1 being the most important races and including the classics

penalty a weight added to the handicap weight of a horse

photo finish a close race where the aid of a photograph is
needed to determine the result

plate a shoe worn by a horse for racing

plater a horse that runs in selling races

pony £25

pulled up a horse that drops out of the race after the off

punter someone who bets

race card a programme for the day's racing

rag a horse with little chance of winning (an outsider)

rating a measure of the performance of a horse on a scale of 0–140; 140 is the highest

ready reckoner a table showing returns for odds to aid the calculation of winnings

reduction factor the percentage that will be deducted from odds on a betting exchange in the event of a withdrawn horse

rule 4 a deduction made from the prices due to the withdrawal of a horse from a race

scratch withdraw a horse from a race

settler person who calculates the payout on a bet

sidewheeler a pacer in harness racing

SP starting price

spread the difference between what a spread betting firm predicts and actual outcome

spread a plate lose a horse shoe

stallion male horse that has retired from racing and is mating mares

starter person responsible for starting the race

steeplechase a race over obstacles

steward a Jockey Club official who is responsible for checking that the rules of racing are followed

stewards' enquiry an inquiry into whether or not the rules of racing have been broken

stud place where horses are bred

stud book a book that contains the pedigree of thoroughbred racehorses

system a method of betting that is supposed to favour the player

thoroughbred a horse bred for racing that is registered in the general stud book

tic-tac hand signals used by bookmakers to communicate price changes

tipster a person employed by a newspaper to recommend horses that are likely to win

tissue prices early prices offered before a betting market has been formed

trip distance of the race

trotter a horse in harness racing that moves with a diagonal gait

under orders race is about to start

up bet or buy in spread betting a bet that the outcome will be higher than the prediction

walkover a race with only one runner. In order to be declared the winner, the horse must walk over the course. Where there are obstacles, the horse need not jump over them, but may walk around

weigh-in after each race the jockeys on the winning and placed horses must weigh in to confirm that they are carrying the same weight as at the start of the race

yearling a horse from 1 January to 31 December of the year following its birth

Taking it further

Gamblers' help organizations

GREAT BRITAIN

GamCare
2 & 3 Baden Place
Crosby Row
London SE1 1YW
Telephone 020 7378 5200
Fax 020 7378 5237
Helpline 0845 6000 133 (24 hour, 7 days a week)
email info@gamcare.org.uk
www.gamcare.org.uk/

UNITED STATES OF AMERICA

Gamblers Intergroup
PO Box 7
New York
New York 10116
Telephone 212 903 4400

AUSTRALIA

Gamblers Anonymous
PO Box 142
Burwood
NSW 1805
Telephone (02) 9564 1574
www.gamblersanonymous.org.au/

Regulatory bodies and arbitration services

British Horseracing Board
Via their website tickets can be purchased for any racing event in
Britain.
www.britishhorseracing.com

The Gambling Commission
www.gamblingcommission.gov.uk/

Financial Services Authority
FSA Consumer Helpline 0845 606 1234 open 8am to 6pm.
The helpline can tell you if a spread betting firm is authorized.
www.fsa.gov.uk/

Interactive Gaming Council Canada
175–2906 West Broadway
Vancouver BC V6K 2G8
Canada
Telephone 604 732 3833
Fax 604 732 3866
www.igcouncil.org/contact.php

Independent Betting Arbitration Service (IBAS)
PO Box 4011
London E14 5BB
www.ibas-uk.com/

Addresses of British racecourses

Aintree Racecourse Co. Ltd
Aintree
Liverpool L9 5AS
www.aintree.co.uk

Ascot Racecourse
Ascot
Berkshire SL5 7JN
www.ascot-authority.co.uk

Ayr Western Meeting Club Racecourse Office
2 Whitletts Road
Ayr KA8 0JE
www.ayr-racecourse.co.uk/

Bangor-on-Dee Races Ltd
The Racecourse
Wrexham LL13 0DA
www.bangordee.co.uk

Bath Racecourse Co. Ltd
Lansdown
Bath BA1 9BU
www.comeracing.co.uk/bath.htm

Beverley Race Co. Ltd
The Racecourse
York Road
Beverley
Yorkshire HU17 8QZ
www.goracing.co.uk/

Brighton Racecourse Co. Ltd
Freshfield Road
Brighton
East Sussex BN2 2XZ
www.brighton-racecourse.co.uk

Carlisle Racecourse Co. Ltd
Durdar Road
Carlisle
Cumbria CA2 4TS
www.carlisle-races.co.uk

Cartmel Steeplechases (Holker) Ltd
Cartmel
Nr Grange-over-Sands
Cumbria LA11 6QF
www.comeracing.co.uk/cartmel.htm

Catterick Racecourse Co. Ltd
Catterick Bridge
Richmond
North Yorkshire DL10 7PE
www.catterickbridge.co.uk

Cheltenham Racecourse
Prestbury Park
Cheltenham GL50 4SH
www.cheltenham.co.uk/

Chepstow Racecourse plc
The Racecourse
Chepstow
Gwent NP6 5YH
www.chepstow-racecourse.co.uk/

Chester Race Co. Ltd
The Racecourse
Cheshire CH1 2LY
www.chester-races.co.uk

Devon and Exeter Steeplechases Ltd
The Racecourse
Halden
Nr Exeter
Devon EX2 4DE
www.comeracing.co.uk/exeter.htm

Doncaster Racecourse
The Grandstand
Leger Way

Doncaster
Yorkshire DN2 6BB
www.doncaster-racecourse.com

Epsom
United Racecourses (Holdings)
The Grandstand
Epsom Downs,
Surrey KT18 5LQ
www.epsomderby.co.uk/

Fakenham Racecourse Ltd
The Racecourse
Fakenham
Norfolk NR21 7NY
www.comeracing.co.uk/fakenham.htm

Folkestone Racecourse plc
Westhanger
Hythe
Kent CT21 4HX
www.folkestone-racecourse.co.uk

Fontwell Park Steeplechase plc
Fontwell
Nr Arundel
West Sussex BN18 0SX
www.fontwellpark.co.uk

Goodwood Racecourse Ltd
Goodwood
Chichester
West Sussex PO18 0PS
www.goodwood.co.uk

Great Yarmouth Racecourse
Jellicoe Road
Great Yarmouth

Norfolk NR30 4AU
www.comeracing.co.uk/yarmouth.htm

The Hamilton Park Race Course Co. Ltd
Bothwell Road
Hamilton
Lanarkshire ML3 0DW
www.hamilton-park.co.uk

Haydock Park Racecourse Co. Ltd
Newton-le-Willows
Merseyside WA12 0HQ
www.haydock-park.com

Hereford Racecourse Co. Ltd
Shepherds Meadow
Eaton Bishop
Hereford HR2 9UA
www.comeracing.co.uk/hereford.htm

Hexham Steeplechase Co. Ltd
The Ridings
Hexham
Northumberland NE46 4PF
www.hexham-racecourse.co.uk/

Huntingdon Steeplechases Ltd
Brampton
Huntingdon
Cambridgeshire PE18 8NN
www.huntingdonracing.co.uk

Kelso Races Ltd Sale & Partners
18/20 Glendale Road
Wooler
Northumberland NE71 6DW
www.kelso-races.co.uk

Kempton
United Racecourses (Holdings) Ltd
Kempton Park Racecourse
Sunbury-on-Thames TW16 5AQ
www.kempton.co.uk/

Leicester Racecourse Co. Ltd
The Racecourse
Oadby
Leicester LE2 4AL
www.comeracing.co.uk/leicester.htm

Lingfield Park (1991) Ltd
Racecourse Road
Lingfield
Surrey RH7 6PQ
www.lingfield-racecourse.co.uk

Ludlow Race Club Ltd
Shepherds Meadow
Eaton Bishop
Hereford HR2 9UA
www.ludlow-racecourse.co.uk

Market Rasen Racecourse Ltd
Legsby Road
Market Rasen
Lincolnshire LN8 3EA
www.marketrasenraces.co.uk

Musselburgh Joint Racing Committee
Linkfield Road
Musselburgh
East Lothian EH21 7RG
www.musselburgh-racecourse.co.uk/

Newbury Racecourse plc
The Racecourse
Newbury
Berkshire RG14 7NZ
www.newbury-racecourse.co.uk

Newcastle
High Gosforth Park Ltd
Newcastle Racecourse
High Gosforth Park
Newcastle upon Tyne NE3 5HP
www.comeracing.co.uk/newcastle.htm

Newmarket Racecourses Trust
Westfield House
Cambridge Road
Newmarket
Suffolk CB8 0TG
www.newmarketracecourses.co.uk/

Newton Abbot Races Ltd
The Racecourse
Kingsteignton Road
Newton Abbot
Devon TQ12 3AF
www.naracecourse.co.uk

Nottingham Racecourse Co. Ltd
Colwick Park
Colwick Road
Nottingham NG2 4BE
www.nottinghamracecourse.co.uk

Perth Hunt Perth Racecourse
Scone Palace Park
Perth PH2 6BB
www.perth-races.co.uk

Plumpton Racecourse Ltd
Plumpton
East Sussex BN7 3AL
www.plumptonracecourse.co.uk

Pontefract Park Race Co. Ltd
33 Ropergate
Pontefract
West Yorkshire WF8 1LE
www.pontefract-races.co.uk

Redcar Racecourse Ltd
The Racecourse
Redcar
Cleveland TS10 2BY
www.redcarracing.co.uk

Ripon Race Co. Ltd.
77 North Street
Ripon
North Yorkshire HG4 1DS
www.goracing.co.uk/detail.htm#ripon

Salisbury
The Bibury Club
Salisbury Racecourse
Netherhampton
Salisbury SP2 8PN
www.salisburyracecourse.co.uk

Sandown
United Racecourse (Holdings) Ltd
The Racecourse
Esher
Surrey KT10 9AJ
www.sandown.co.uk/

Sedgefield Steeplechase Co. (1927) Ltd
The Racecourse
Sedgefield
Stockton-on-Tees
Cleveland TS21 2HW
www.comeracing.co.uk/sedgefield.htm

Southwell
RAM Racecourses Ltd
Rolleston
Southwell
Nottinghamshire NG25 0TS
www.southwell-racecourse.co.uk

Stratford on Avon Racecourse Co. Ltd
Luddington Road
Stratford upon Avon CV37 9SE
www.stratfordracecourse.net

Taunton Racecourse Co. Ltd
Orchard Portman
Taunton
Somerset TA3 7BL
www.tauntonracecourse.co.uk

Thirsk Racecourse Ltd
Station Road
Thirsk
North Yorkshire YO7 1QL
www.goracing.co.uk/detail.htm#thirsk

Towcester Racecourse Co. Ltd
Easton Neston
Towcester
Northamptonshire NN12 7HS
www.towcester-racecourse.co.uk

Uttoxeter Leisure and Development Co. Ltd
The Racecourse
Wood Lane
Uttoxeter
Staffordshire ST14 8BD
www.uttoxeterracecourse.co.uk

Warwick Racecourse
Hampton Street
Warwick CV34 6HN
www.warwickracecourse.co.uk

Wetherby Steeplechase Committee Ltd
The Racecourse
York Road
Wetherby
North Yorkshire LS22 5 EJ
www.wetherbyracing.co.uk

Wincanton Races Co. Ltd
The Racecourse
Wincanton
Somerset BA9 8BJ
www.wincantonracecourse.co.uk

Windsor Racing Ltd
The Racecourse
Windsor
Berkshire SL4 5JJ
www.windsorracing.co.uk

Wolverhampton
Dunstall Park Centre Ltd
Gorsebrook Road
Wolverhampton WV6 0PE
www.wolverhampton-racecourse.co.uk

Worcester Racecourse
Grandstand Road
Pitchcroft
Worcester WR1 3EJ
www.worcester-racecourse.co.uk

York Race Committee
The Racecourse
York
Yorkshire YO23 1EX
www.yorkracecourse.co.uk

UK bookmakers

Coral
www.coral.co.uk/

Ladbrokes
www.ladbrokes.com/

Paddy Power
www.paddypower.com/

Totesport
www.totesport.com/

Tote Ireland
www.tote.ie/

Victor Chandler
www.vcbet.com/

William Hill
www.willhill.com/

Betting exchanges

Betfair
www.betfair.com/

Betdaq
www.betdaq.co.uk/

GG-Bet
www.gg.com/

Spread betting firms

Sporting Index
www.sportingindex.com/

SportsSpread.com
www.sportsspread.com/

SpreadEx
www.spreadex.com/

Horse racing publications

GREAT BRITAIN

In the Know
Monthly horse racing magazine.
www.itkonline.com/

Inside Edge
Monthly magazine covering all forms of gambling.
www.inside-edge-mag.co.uk/

Pacemaker
www.pacemakerworld.com/

Raceform
Publishers of horse racing information, including the official
formbook and three weekly newspapers:

Racing & Football Outlook – weekly preview of forthcoming
racing and football fixtures with tips and statistics.

Raceform Update – racing data, expert analysis and tips for racing.

Weekend Special – tips for weekend racing.
www.raceform.co.uk/

Racing Ahead
Monthly horse racing magazine aimed at punters.
www.racingahead.net/

Racing Post
Daily newspaper.
www.racingpost.co.uk/

Timeform
Publishers of horse racing publications including *Timeform Race
Cards*, the weekly *Timeform Black Book*, *Racehorses*, *Chasers &
Hurdlers*, *Timeform Perspective*, *Computer Timeform* and
Timeform Horses to Follow.
www.timeform.com/

UNITED STATES OF AMERICA

American Turf Monthly
Thoroughbred handicapping magazine.
www.americanturf.com/

The Blood-Horse
Monthly magazine.
services.bloodhorse.com/

Daily Racing Form
www.drf.com/

Thoroughbred Times
Weekly magazine.
www.thoroughbredtimes.com/

CANADA

The Canadian Sportsman
Biweekly harness racing publication.
www.canadiansportsman.ca/

Trot Magazine
Monthly magazine.
www.standardbredcanada.ca/

AUSTRALIA AND NEW ZEALAND

Australasian Turf Monthly
www.americanturf.com/

Harness Racing New Zealand
www.hrnz.co.nz/

SOUTH AFRICA

Sporting Post
www.sportingpost.co.za/

THE GULF

RaceWeek
www.raceweek.co.uk/

Index

Image credits